CONCISE GUIDE TO

LIBRARY
RESEARCH

ABOUT THE AUTHOR

Grant W. Morse received his B. A. at Ottawa University, Kansas, his M. S. in Library Science at the State University of New York at Albany, and a M. Div. from E. B. T. S., Philadelphia, Pa.

Mr. Morse is a member of the American Association of University Professors and of the Association of University of Wisconsin Faculties. He has been Assistant Librarian at Carthage College and Head Librarian at Findlay College, Ottawa University, Grove City College, Wagner College, and since 1966, at the University of Wisconsin Center-Barron County, Rice Lake, Wisconsin. Mr. Morse has also authored: Complete Guide to Organizing and Documenting Research Papers, 1974, and Filing Rules for a Three-Way Divided Card Catalog, 1971.

CONCISE GUIDE TO

LIBRARY
RESEARCH

by Grant W. Morse

Head Librarian
University of Wisconsin Center
Barron County, Rice, Lake, Wisconsin

FLEET ACADEMIC EDITIONS, INC.
New York

DEDICATION

To my son, Kendall Grant and daughter, Gail Evonne

PREFACE

Library research can be as exciting as scuba diving for sunken treasure. But many do not know where the treasure is, whether on the ocean floor or the third floor of the library stacks.

A student has not been in an academic high school or a college long before he realizes that his library is more than a place to check out Mailer's latest novel. There will be assigned readings, and there will be research problems.

How does one solve these problems? How does one research? I hope this guide will help answer these questions. Detailed knowledge of library science is relevant only to librarians, and I wish to avoid such a presentation here. I hope to show the inexperienced college student how the library can help him crystallize his topic, proceed toward his general area of information, and focus at last on his own specific data.

The guide is divided into three sections, beginning with KEY TO RESEARCH—basic procedural orientation. KEY TO REFERENCE BOOKS summarizes standard reference works and lists those in various fields as well. KEY TO PERIODICALS outlines by subject the major publications the student will encounter.

To facilitate the finding of specific reference works, each subject has been assigned a code number. The code numbers were formed by giving a letter to each main section under KEY TO REFERENCE BOOKS: "A" to the Basic General Reference Works, and "B" to Basic Reference Works in Various Fields. The subject entries are numbered consecutively.

The materials in this book were originally written with the college student in mind. However, there is no reason why most, if not all, of this book should not apply to the very analogous problems of the average high school student in a college-preparatory course.

Most students are unaware of how much a library can help them in their class work and personal interest, as well as, research. The variety of reference books listed in this guide is intended to provide an overview of types of information available in a good library. Hopefully, you will find this guide a quick reference to the location of materials and will use it repeatedly throughout your schooling.

The list of reference books is selective with no intention of being all-inclusive. However, you will find here some of the best and most useful works available in libraries. These basic books are not useful only to the beginning student; good reference works are of lasting value.

Most students will have little need for detailed information about each title listed in this guide—such knowledge is for the advanced subject specialist or student of Library Science. Rather, this guide is a starting point to locate information you need.

The student is led consecutively from the broad subject area, subdivision, to titles—usually sufficient (or the maximum to which most students have immediate interest) to place him in the appropriate reference work. Regardless of the amount of information given to an annotation, initially the student may need help from a reference librarian. After this first encounter, detailed annotations become burdensome to the quick reference use for which this guide is designed—to be used repeatedly.

The Library of Congress classification number has been added to this edition as a further aid for the student in locating the volume. Although the exact classification number given to a title may vary between libraries, usually the difference will be so minor as not to make location impossible. In libraries not using the Library of Congress classification system, you should consult the card catalog.

The subject index at the end of the guide will enable you to turn quickly to the general or specific subject of your interest.

I would like to thank the many librarians, faculty members and students who have contributed helpful suggestions for this guide.

Special thanks to Mr. Thomas Fitz for his many suggestions.

My thanks go also to those who helped type the manuscript and to my wife, Jocelyn, who has given assistance and encouragement throughout this endeavor.

G.W.M.

August, 1975

CONTENTS

KEY TO RESEARCH

Where Do I Start Digging?

Finding the Treasure

KEY TO REFERENCE BOOKS

KEY TO PERIODICALS

APPENDIX

KEY TO RESEARCH

Where Do I Start Digging?

The following brief topics suggest a typical pattern of questions the student should ask as he seeks to solve research problems. No attempt is made here to deal with subject content, organization, or note taking, only with the elements of beginning, self-questioning, and searching for materials. These are the first stepping stones across the ocean of research. Without a plan to follow, either conscious or unconscious, the student is sure to be swept under the tide. (See: B22a for Documentation and Organizing of a research paper).

The next section, KEY TO REFERENCE BOOKS takes the student a step further by narrowing the search, focusing and directing him to materials within the scope of his inquiry.

HOW DO I CHOOSE MY SUBJECT?

The first problem confronting the beginner in research is the choice of a subject. Basic considerations are as follows:

1. Choose a topic you like.

2. Choose a topic that you can handle in the time and word length allotted for the paper. The most prevalent tendency of inexperienced writers is to undertake a subject with too broad a scope. The tendency in the search for materials is to expand the subject too much as the investigation proceeds, necessitating a contraction of the original statement later.
3. Choose a topic that you are qualified to undertake.
4. Avoid inappropriate subjects, for example, those centered on matters of taste or personal opinion, which cannot be established through the techniques of research.
   (*Example:* "Why——is the greatest author who ever lived.")
   Also, topics based on "how to" do something may restrict your source materials to only one or two sources, which is not enough for a research paper.
5. If you have no idea what subject to choose, suggested topics may be found by glancing through the card catalog, *The Readers' Guide to Periodical Literature*, encyclopedias, periodicals, dictionaries, and the like.

HOW DO I NARROW MY SUBJECT?

So much has been written about science, religion, art, literature, and history that the problem of narrowing one's subject is often vexing. Three suggestions for narrowing a topic are given here. The field of history will be used to illustrate the first method.

1. If your area of interest is United States history, turn to the History section under KEY TO REFERENCE BOOKS, B139–162. Look under the United States for "General Works." Find one or two of these volumes on the shelf (Usually they will all be found together).
2. The arrangement of the headings in these volumes will often provide a natural breakdown of topics.
3. Take the Civil War, for example. You could cut the material in half simply by focusing on either the North or the South.
4. Note subdivisions under the Civil War, such as "Military and Naval Operations." A glance through the paragraphs below such a heading will suggest further subdivisions, such as "The Methods of Recruitment" or "Undercover Activities." Even one of these may be subdivided if you begin to find too much material.

This same procedure may be followed even when the general topic is assigned. Note the following example:

U.S.—HISTORY (Area of interest)

 CIVIL WAR (Subject too large)

  THE SOUTH AND THE CIVIL WAR (Subject too large)

  ECONOMIC CONSEQUENCES OF THE CIVIL WAR (Subject too large)

   Trade in cotton during the Civil War
   Reconstruction
   War losses
   Plantation system

  MILITARY AND NAVAL OPERATIONS (Subject too large)

   Methods of recruitment
   The Merrimac
   A chronology of events
   Undercover activities

  POLITICAL (Subject too large)

   Causes of Civil War
   Confederate diplomacy
   Reaction to Lincoln

  MISCELLANEOUS SUBJECTS (Subject too large)

   Propaganda
   Emancipation Proclamation
   Consequences if the war had not been fought

A second means of narrowing a topic for a research paper is by using the card catalog:

1. If your area of interest is drama, look in the card catalog under the subject DRAMA. Unless your library is very small, you will find many cards with the subject heading DRAMA at the top. This is a sure indication that DRAMA in itself is too large a topic.
2. Subdivisions or phrase subject headings after DRAMA may prove useful for some topics, but they will probably also be too large:

DRAMA—HISTORY AND CRITICISM
DRAMA IN EDUCATION

3. Depending on your knowledge of the general subject DRAMA, you may need to turn to a general work on this subject (listed under Literature in the KEY TO REFERENCE BOOKS), or a general encyclopedia (A1).
   Either of these may suggest the limiting of your topic to a specific dramatist, a type of drama, a single play, or the like.
4. If you use Shakespeare as an example and turn again to the card catalog, you will find too many cards with this subject heading:

SHAKESPEARE—AUTHORSHIP
SHAKESPEARE—STYLE

5. You might single out one of Shakespeare's works, for example "Macbeth," and focus on it. This would still be too large a subject for a paper; therefore, you could consider a person in the work or an aspect of it, or compare two aspects or discuss the work's symbolism.
6. Under the subject heading SHAKESPEARE—BIOGRAPHIES, you might write on an aspect of that poet's life.

   The following example may help you visualize how to narrow your topic by using the card catalog:

DRAMA (Area of interest)
   Look in card catalog under DRAMA. (Subject too large)

   Look at subdivisions of DRAMA

DRAMA—HISTORY AND CRITICISM ⎫
DRAMA—TECHNIQUE   ⎬ **Subjects Too large**
DRAMA IN EDUCATION   ⎭

SHAKESPEARE (Restricting subject by dramatist, still too large)

Subdivisions
    SHAKESPEARE—AUTHOR-
    SHIP

    SHAKESPEARE—STAGE HISTORY   }   **Subjects too large**

    SHAKESPEARE—STYLE

One of Shakespeare's single works

    MACBETH (Subject too large)
    "The development of Lady Macbeth's passion to kill"
    (Possible topic for paper)
  SHAKESPEARE—BIOGRAPHIES
    "Shakespeare's economic success" (Possible topic for
    paper)

Another means of restricting your subject is to observe how others have handled it. Glancing at the topics used for dissertations is the easiest approach (see dissertations, B22). Although you are not writing a dissertation, such titles will often suggest a method for limiting your topic. Furthermore, you might get a kick out of reading the subjects others have chosen: "A Comparative Study of Three Bootblacks," "The Use of Humor in the Fiction of W. D. Howells," "The Dialect of Tom Sawyer."

Note that the following discussion (How Do I Approach My Subject?) may also serve as a natural means of restricting the subject.

HOW DO I APPROACH MY SUBJECT?

It is easier to select a topic if you are aware of several different approaches to the problem. Even when the topic is assigned, one of the following approaches, or a combination of these, may make the topic easier or more interesting:

BIBLIOGRAPHICAL: A collection of resource material relating to a specific subject, author, or period. The list may be complete or selective. Brief descriptive or evaluative notes may be given with each work listed.

    Example: Make a list of books and articles on college dating. Include an evaluation on the way each has helped you.

BIOGRAPHICAL: Factual information about the history of a person's life. This approach does not usually present all aspects of an individual's life.

Example: Write on the early years of Pithecanthropus up to the time he became famous for his treetop swing.

CHRONOLOGICAL: An account of events in the order of time. The arrangment of the data or events in order of occurrence or appearance may cover current or historical information.

Example: Cover the highlights of the Pessimist Club.

GEOGRAPHICAL: Limits the topic to a given area, location, or place—a descriptive treatment. It may also refer to the distribution of plant and animal life, including man and his industries.

Example: Write about the growth and development of Standstill Village during the Depression.

LINGUISTIC: The study of language's nature, development, and origin.

Example: Trace the origin and meaning of some slang terms connected with automobiles, such as "drag race."

PRACTICAL: The application of knowledge to some useful end. Such an approach is designed to supplement the purely theoretical view. It applies to both things and people—the actual life and the useful, serviceable, practical result.

Example: Practical uses made of Russian refugee newspapers.

STATISTICAL: The collection, analysis, interpretation, and presentation of masses of numerical data.

Example: A compilation of data of the New York municipal elections of 1975.

THEORETICAL: Deals with the inferences drawn from observed facts and the results of experiments.

Example: The probable effects of weightlessness on birds in outer space.

HOW DO I DETERMINE WHICH TYPE SOURCE TO USE?

1. Make use of a variety of sources in gathering your material. This

may eliminate some topics or ways of treating a subject, depending on the materials available in your library.

2. Since very few primary sources are available to the college student, printed autobiographies, reprints of historical documents, interviews, questionnaires, diaries, manuscripts, journals, and letters may be regarded as primary. If you wish to know what St. Paul thought, read what St. Paul wrote, not what somebody else says he thought.

3. For many topics secondary sources may comprise the major part of your research: these are materials that have been reported, analyzed, or interpreted by other persons. Secondary works are often helpful in indicating what the primary sources are, in interpreting and criticizing them, in establishing the facts, and in synthesizing them. There are three dangers in using secondary sources: (a) you may be swayed by the opinions of your secondary authority and take his view of the subject; (b) this may lead to lack of confidence in your own opinion; and (c) your work may lack authority.

4. All important statements from primary or secondary sources must be placed within quotation marks and their locations cited.

5. Your interpretation, evaluation, and judgment should be injected into your research paper. (See also the section on How to Evaluate Books.)

6. Next, you must choose the means to find the needed materials. The major part of this guide is devoted to this purpose.

HOW DO I SELECT SPECIFIC SOURCES?

1. Know clearly just what you need: statistics, general information, the amount of information, current data, biographical materials, and such. Thirty minutes of thought spent here will save you hours of searching.

2. Whenever possible, start with general works in your subject field or general encyclopedias to get a survey and background of the topic—names, dates, location, bibliography, and so forth. By their nature, general works are more apt to include different points of view and to summarize them in a more impartial manner.

3. The inexperienced researcher must rely largely on selective and/or evaluative bibliographies. (See those listed under various fields in the KEY TO REFERENCE BOOKS.) Annotated bibliographies are most valuable. Always remember that just because a book is listed in the library card catalog, it does not follow that the book has any particular value. Therefore, selective and specialized bibliographies are essential.

HOW DO I LOCATE BOOKS
IN THE STACKS?

Approach the card catalog with discrimination, imagination, and alertness. It is not an obstacle to be avoided whenever possible, nor is it as simple as ABC. The following points on the card catalog will aid you in using most libraries:

1. Why use the card catalog at all?
   a. The card catalog is an index to the book collection in your library, just as a map is a guide to a given location. The card catalog is an alphabetical list of cards, representing books, filed by author, title, and subject, together with information on the location of the book on the shelves.
   b. With closed stacks the card catalog is a must. With open stacks it saves time and guards against one's overlooking important books whose locations may be widely separated on the shelves.
   c. The title *The Pink Slip* may suggest a dime store novel, but this title was given to a book on dismissal of employees. It shows that, even when searching the shelf, you may overlook a book because of the title and miss the very material you need. In the card catalog, the subject cards representing the book ignore the title and give the book's basic content.
   d. A close look at the catalog card will *help* you to decide whether the book it represents is the one you want. (See page 24)
   e. Especially note the call number on the catalog card. Most libraries have a few special collections shelved separately from the main collection of books. The call number will indicate where these books are shelved.

2. Learning a few of the catalog filing practices will greatly facilitate your searches for material. Although the cards are filed in the catalog alphabetically by author, title, and subject, special filing rules are necessary.

   The following are some of the important rules for author and title cards. (See point 3 for those on subjects.)

SAMPLE CATALOG CARDS FOR THE SAME BOOK

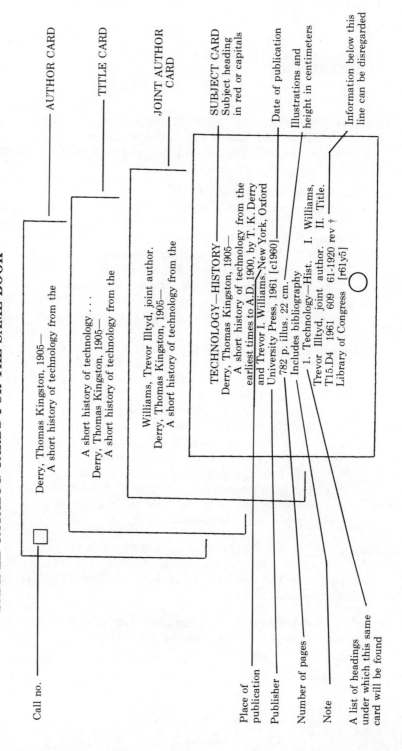

AUTHOR CARD

Derry, Thomas Kingston, 1905—
   A short history of technology from the

TITLE CARD

A short history of technology . . .
Derry, Thomas Kingston, 1905—
   A short history of technology from the

JOINT AUTHOR CARD

Williams, Trevor Illtyd, joint author.
Derry, Thomas Kingston, 1905—
   A short history of technology from the

SUBJECT CARD
Subject heading
in red or capitals

TECHNOLOGY—HISTORY
Derry, Thomas Kingston, 1905—
   A short history of technology from the
earliest times to A.D. 1900, by T. K. Derry
and Trevor I. Williams. New York, Oxford
University Press, 1961 [c1960]
   782 p. illus. 22 cm.
   Includes bibliography

   1. Technology—Hist.   I. Williams,
Trevor Illtyd, joint author.   II. Title.
T15.D4 1961 609 61-1920 rev †
Library of Congress [r61y5]

Date of publication

Illustrations and
height in centimeters

Information below this
line can be disregarded

Call no.

Place of
publication

Publisher

Number of pages

Note

A list of headings
under which this same
card will be found

a. Articles—When the first word of title is an article (a, an, the, *le*, *les*, *un*, *une*, *der*, *das*, *die*), it is disregarded in the filing. This rule applies to articles in all languages.

The *man*

*M*an and nature

A *m*an in a tree

b. Abbreviations—Abbreviations are arranged as though they were spelled out in some libraries.

Dr., Doctor

St., Saint

c. M', Mc, and Mac—Words beginning with these are either filed as though they were all spelled *Mac* or as spelt.

*Mc*Laren, A. B.	*Mac* Loren, D. B.
*M'*Laren, B. B.	*Mc* Loren, A. B.
*Mc*Laren, C. B.	*Mc* Loren, C. B.
*Mac*Laren, D. B.	*M'* Loren, B. B.

d. Numerals—These are filed as though spelled out.

1920, Nineteen twenty

100 Stories, One Hundred Stories

1720, Seventeen twenty

e. Organizations as authors—An "author" may be an institution, a government, an organization, or a society, and may be found under a heading such as:

American Anthropological Association

New York (State) Legislature

U. S. Department of State

3. Why doesn't the library have anything on my topic? Finding the wanted subject in the card catalog is much like looking for hidden treasure: you may come very close but not find what you want. Be especially watchful of subject headings.

a. The four basic types of subject headings are given below:

Without Divisions:

ART

With Subdivisions:

ART—OBJECTS

ART—OBJECTS—CATALOGS (special subdivision)

ART—BERLIN (geographical subdivision)

ART—HISTORY—20th CENTURY (period subdivision)

ART—1945 (period subdivision)
Inverted Subject Headings:
ART, AMERICAN
Phrase Subject Heading:
ART AND MORALS

Some libraries use a period in place of a dash for subdivision: ART.
HISTORY.

b. In the following arrangement, the subdivision cards are filed
alphabetically beginning at the top. The period division
headings are arranged chronologically following the
subdivision cards, the oldest period first. The following
subdivision examples represent the cards in the order you
would find them filed in the card catalog.

U.S.—HISTORY

U.S.—HISTORY—POETRY

U.S.—HISTORY—STUDY AND
TEACHING

} Special subdivisions

U.S.—HISTORY—REVOLUTION

U.S.—HISTORY—CIVIL WAR

U.S.—HISTORY—1940–1947

} Period divisions (chronological by period)

c. The subject examples are in the order you would find the cards
filed in the card catalog, strictly alphabetically:

ART, AFRICAN

ART, DECORATIVE

ART, ENGLISH

ART, GOTHIC

ART, ROMAN

d. These same cards may also be arranged alphabetically in
groups of the general subject:

ART, DECORATIVE

ART, GOTHIC

} Alphabetical by type

ART, AFRICAN
ART, ENGLISH   } Alphabetical by country
ART, ROMAN

e. The following illustrates the typical arrangement of all four types of subject headings as they would appear in the card catalog.

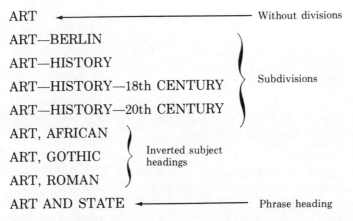

ART ◄——————————————— Without divisions

ART—BERLIN
ART—HISTORY
ART—HISTORY—18th CENTURY   } Subdivisions
ART—HISTORY—20th CENTURY

ART, AFRICAN
ART, GOTHIC   } Inverted subject headings
ART, ROMAN

ART AND STATE ◄——————————— Phrase heading

The arrangement of the examples given above is not always the same in every library. But with these basic arrangements in mind, you are not likely to pass over or fall short of the information you seek.

4. How do I look for a subject in the card catalog? If you are looking for the subject, BATTLE OF GETTYSBURG, 1863:
   a. Look under GETTYSBURG, BATTLE OF, 1863. You may also find cards such as GETTYSBURG CAMPAIGN, 1863.
   b. If you find nothing under either of these subject headings, look under the next broader topic that would include your subject: PENNSYLVANIA—HISTORY—CIVIL WAR; or U.S.—HISTORY—CIVIL WAR.
   The broader the subject of the book, the more necessary it becomes to use the book's index and/or table of contents.
   c. If the subject heading you are looking for cannot be found, look under a similar one:

Your Subject	Look Under
Gallup Polls	Public Opinion Polls
Betting	Gambling
Oil	Petroleum

If available, the *Subject Headings Used in the Dictionary Catalogs of the Library of Congress* is most helpful in finding the proper subject heading to look under.

Another helpful guide to subject headings you are looking for is the *Cross-Reference Index*, 1974, Bowker (Z695.A94). This is a list of subject headings used in six major information sources. This index aids the user to tell the various subject headings used in these sources for the same topic.

5. The Dewey Decimal and the Library of Congress are the two systems of classification used most by libraries. For a brief summary of each system, see pages 210–216.
6. See point 5 under HOW DO I USE BOOKS TO THE BEST ADVANTAGE below for the two basic kinds of alphabetical arrangements also used in card catalogs.
7. Don't give up on the card catalog—ask your Reference Librarian for help.

HOW DO I USE BOOKS
TO THE BEST ADVANTAGE?

1. When you find material on your topic, be sure to write down the identifying information—page, volume, date, name of book or periodical, author, and so forth.
2. Always use the index and the table of contents of a book.
3. Read the introduction to each reference book at least once.
4. Look for appendixes—they are often valuable.
5. Two basic kinds of alphabetical arrangements are used in reference works:

WORD-BY-WORD

Wash	(Wash)
Wash basins	(Wash basins)
Wash tubs	(Wash tubs)
Washer solvent	(Washer solvent)
Washers	(Washers)
Washing	(Washing)
Washington	(Washington)

LETTER-BY-LETTER

Wash	(Wash)
Wash basins	(Washbasins)
Washers	(Washers)
Washer solvent	(Washersolvent)
Washing	(Washing)
Washington	(Washington)
Wash tubs	(Washtubs)

When alphabetizing word-by-word, all like separate words (in this case "wash") which introduce a phrase will follow each other consecutively. They will be alphabetized by the word following (note the first three words in the above Word-by-Word list). In the parenthesis following each word or phrase, the letter on which you are to alphabetize is underlined.

However, when alphabetizing letter-by-letter, you disregard the separate words and assume the phrase to be just one long word. This is indicated in the parenthesis following each word in the above Letter-by-Letter list. The letter being alphabetized on is underlined. You will notice that the phrase "wash tubs" is last in the Letter-by-Letter list and third in the Word-by-Word list.

Knowing these two basic arrangements of alphabetizing of words and phrases may keep you from overlooking needed materials in book indexes, periodical indexes, and the library card catalog. It is to be noted that books, etc. do not normally indicate to the user which type of alphabetizing they are using—it's up to you to know the difference and find out which they are using.

6. Understanding the various parts of a book will save you much time in determining whether a book will be useful to you. When using books, look particularly for:
   a. Title: Distinguishing name of book.
   b. Author, editor, or compiler: Name of person responsible for preparation of book's contents. Watch for note listing author's degrees and such.
   c. Edition: Indicates how often book has been revised.
   d. Publishing dates and copyright date: Copyright date is more dependable. It suggests recency or obsolescence of material.
   e. Publisher: May suggest authority, viewpoint, or the standards to be expected.
   f. Preface and/or foreword: Author's purpose.
   g. Introduction: Statement of the book's subject and its treatment by the author—sometimes appears as first chapter of book.
   h. Table of contents: Bird's-eye view of book's structure and content.
   i. Index: Locates particular names and subjects quickly. It is usually best to start here when looking for a specific subject.
   j. Appendixes: Glossaries, tables, and such—often as important as rest of the book.
   k. Illustrations: The joy of the slow reader. May be as important as the text.
   l. Reading list, bibliographies, and footnotes: Often give authority for author's statements and lead you to additional material on same subject.

Do not believe every word you read—all authors are human and capable of error and prejudice. Out-of-date books may be useless except as historical studies. However, not all truth, not all that is most valuable or most authoritative, is contained in the most recent books. Sometimes we must rely on those great classics of the past, which seem never to run dry. Read critically and thoughtfully. Be alert for the truth.

HOW DO I EVALUATE BOOKS?

1. General factors to be considered with most books:
   a. Is the author qualified in scholarship, experience on the

subject about which he is writing? Is he familiar with his subject personally?

b. What is his personal attitude toward his book? Does he display strong opinions, partisanship, prejudice?

c. Is the material well expressed? Is the literary style creative, forceful, graceful?

d. Are the authorities used cited fully, accurately, and carefully?

e. Is the work a conscientious presentation of all available facts?

f. Is there some reason for its existence, is it of value to anyone?

g. Is the book written for the scholar and specialist, or for the general reader?

h. Does the subject show intellectual discrimination? Is it clearly and carefully organized, and well-proportioned?

i. Is the content of the book complete or partial, exhaustive or condensed?

j. Is the book authoritative: is it based on original or good secondary sources, or both?

k. What are the strongest and weakest features of the work?

l. What is the contribution to knowledge in its subject?

m. Is the format good: table of contents, full and accurate indexes, illustrations, appendixes, authorities cited, bibliographies, notes?

n. How does your evaluation of the work compare with that of others?

o. Does the author stand to gain by my believing him; is he writing to prove a point just for personal or corporate gain?

2. Additional factors in subject areas:

Biography

AUTOBIOGRAPHY

a. Is the book honest, simple, and, above all, interesting?

b. Is the book a "firsthand" creation or was it prepared by a so-called "ghost-writer"?

BIOGRAPHY

a. Is the author accurate, sympathetic, and impartial?

b. Is the book well-balanced, or is it gossipy and disconnected?

c. Is the author biased, or is this definitely a critical biography fairly presented?

d. Does the author have an understanding of human nature?

e. Is the individual subject interesting in himself, or was he made interesting by the art of the biographer?
f. Is the book fictionalized: is there constant use of the present tense in narrative; is there constant introduction of dialogue and a highly pictorial rendering of dramatic or emotional scenes?
g. Was the biography written during the lifetime of the subject? If so, it may be of less value.

History

GENERAL HISTORY

a. Note the type of historical writing; is it narrative and descriptive, philosophical, critical, social; or does it overlap and merge among the types?
b. Is the format good: maps, genealogical or chronological tables, full and accurate indexes, illustrations and portraits, citations from authorities, bibliographies, notes, and references?

TRAVEL

a. Is the author qualified? Are his observations precise or just hasty impressions; is he an experienced traveler or an armchair adventurer; does he have special training or authority?
b. Is the writer biased or prejudiced toward the places he depicts?
c. Is the subject interesting in itself or made interesting by the writer's craft?
d. Is the work factual or romantic?

Literature

a. Literature stands or falls not on the writer's academic attainments but on its art.
b. Does the author depict life realistically?
c. Does the writer show insight into human nature?
d. What type of work is this: narrative, fantasy, satire, irony?
e. Does the book contain enough to make it worth your while?

f. Does the book affect you wholesomely; does it stimulate, provoke thought, satisfy, amuse, inspire?
g. Is the plot presented well?
h. Does the book compare well with classics of the same kind?

Philosophy

a. Does the author show originality and creative insight?
b. Does the author express himself well; is he clear?

Religion

Primitive religion: Also see suggested evaluation under science.

Non-Christian and Christian Religions:
a. The authority of the religious writer will depend partly on his theological background and education.
b. Does the writer present all sides fairly, or does he ignore other points of view?
c. Is the author overly critical of other points of view?
d. Does the writer force interpretations in order to fit them into an already established pattern?
e. Is the archaeological data reliable in older books?

Science

a. What are the author's qualifications?
b. Does the work represent firsthand research, experimentation, or observation?
c. Is the work readable and interesting?
d. Is the work logically organized?
e. Does the work summarize, expound a theory, analyze or criticize, record, express a particular point of view, or appeal to a particular group of readers?
f. Is the material up-to-date? Note copyright date and edition of book itself, also copyright dates and editions of materials used in bibliography.
g. Who is the publisher? Those of first rank as a rule conform to high standards.

Social Sciences (Political Science, Sociology, Economics, Education, and Business)

a. Does the author show forcefulness and clarity?
b. Is the author an extremist? Is he dogmatic or intolerant?
c. Is the work theoretical or practical?
d. Do the facts give insight, confuse, become too prolix, or exaggerate the subject?

HOW DO I FIND THE NEWEST AND MOST UP-TO-DATE MATERIAL?

1. The most recent, and perhaps only, material on your topic will be found in periodicals and newspapers and pamphlets (see the following point 6). Just as the card catalog is an index to books, the periodical indexes direct you to periodical material. These indexes are arranged alphabetically by author, subject and title (when necessary).
2. The indexes are usually about two months behind, so it will be necessary to look in the current periodicals themselves for the most recent articles (see KEY TO PERIODICALS).

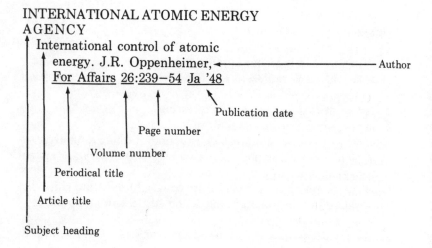

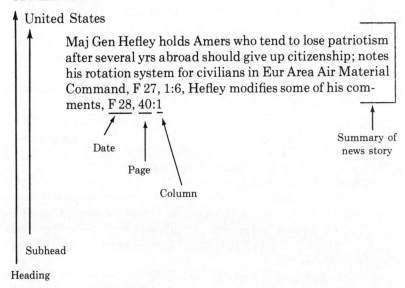

CITIZENSHIP

United States

Maj Gen Hefley holds Amers who tend to lose patriotism after several yrs abroad should give up citizenship; notes his rotation system for civilians in Eur Area Air Material Command, F 27, 1:6, Hefley modifies some of his comments, F 28, 40:1

Date

Page

Column

Summary of news story

Subhead

Heading

3. The example given on page 34 is similar to that in all periodical indexes. See pages 200-209 for excerpts from various indexes.

4. *The New York Times Index* varies from the other periodical indexes as indicated above. Sunday-edition sections, except the first, are indicated by Roman numerals following the date, as: D 25, IV, 4:1. If further information is needed on how to use *The New York Times Index*, it will be found in the front of each annual index.

5. *Facts on File* is a weekly eight to ten page news digest, covering world, national, and foreign affairs, Latin American news, economics, arts and sciences, education and religion, sports, obituaries, and miscellaneous items. News coverage is without comment or bias and covers all the vital news of the week. The cumulative indexes make for rapid pinpointing of current events.

6. Pamphlets are also excellent sources of recent information or opinion on a subject. Pamphlets often cover material not found in either books or periodicals. With the use of the *Vertical-File Index,* you can sometimes send for free or inexpensive informa-

tion on a subject. The *Vertical-File Index* is published monthly and lists booklets, leaflets, and pamphlets currently available from a wide variety of sources.

7. A more recent source of current information, which should not be overlooked, may be found in non-print format. This material may be in the form of audio cassettes, video cassettes, or records. Ask your librarian for help in this area as these materials may not be listed in the card catalog but in a special location.

HOW DO I OBTAIN MATERIALS
OUTSIDE THIS LIBRARY?

The card catalog of any library is only a starter in research. Specific theses, books, and other materials not available at your library may be secured through "interlibrary loan" from another library. Complete information on books and materials desired must be given the librarian, including the full name of the author, title, place, edition, date, and publisher. The carrying charges must be paid by the borrower.

The chief aids in finding additional lists of books by a given author or subject are given below and are essential for securing interlibrary loans:

1. *Cumulative Book Index:* A world list of books in the English language, 1928 to date. (The *C.B.I.* supplements the *U.S. Catalog,* which lists books in print on January 1, 1928.) Both works list by author, title, and subject.
2. *Bibliographic Index:* 1938 to date. A guide to further bibliographies. Good for current bibliographies.
3. *The Library of Congress catalogs:* Issued under various titles; now called *The National Union Catalog.* "It constitutes a reference and research tool for a large part of the world's production of significant books as acquired and cataloged by the Library of Congress and a number of other North American libraries. . . . contains entries for books, pamphlets, maps, atlases, periodicals, and other serials" (from introduction to *The National Union Catalog*).

If you still need help, ask one of the librarians. A reference librarian can be of inestimable help to both beginner and scholar. The unaccustomed user of libraries should readily seek assistance from reference librarians. See: HOW TO GET THE MOST HELP FROM REFERENCE LIBRARIANS.

HOW DO I OUTLINE MY RESEARCH PROCEDURE?

A sure method of research procedure would certainly be ideal, but such is not possible. The following is a suggested outline that will fit most cases and probably bring you to your information in the shortest time. The procedure is organized from the general to the specific and from older to newer materials:

1. Define your subject, turning to dictionaries and general works for basic facts if at all possible.
2. Pursue these basic facts.
3. Bibliographies given with these general works are usually the more important ones and would be well to pursue. Larger bibliographies, although important, may not be selective enough and may include much that is not pertinent. Those bibliographies that are annotated are most important and helpful.
4. The card catalog can prove helpful even when there is nothing specifically mentioned on your subject. Look under the next broader subject. This may prove more helpful.
5. Periodical indexes would be the next logical source. If your subject involves only current material, skip steps 3 and 4 because most of the books will be out of date.
6. Search the pamphlet files, and ask for help if it is needed.
7. If basic works are not found in your library, use another by means of interlibrary loan. The following outline summarizes this procedure.

WORKING OUTLINE I

This outline illustrates the steps in library research that usually prove most profitable.

THE CHAUTAUQUA MOVEMENT (your subject)

Dictionaries, A7* and those under subject areas

Encyclopedias, A1 and general works under subject areas
Dates—Yearbooks, A2—A3

People—Biographical sources, A5—A6

Bibliography —Library Card Catalog

*Numbers refer to KEY TO REFERENCE BOOKS.

LOOK UNDER (in card catalog)

Specific subject or person

Works mentioned in bibliography

Broader subject (in this case: U.S.–HISTORY; NEW YORK (STATE)–HISTORY; etc.)

Periodical Indexes, A4, or under subject fields

LOOK UNDER SPECIFIC SUBJECT OR PERSON

International Index

Education Index

Readers' Guide

Pamphlet file

Ask librarian for suggestions (See: HOW TO GET THE MOST HELP FROM REFERENCE LIBRARIANS).

Interlibrary loan

See: HOW DO I EVALUATE BOOKS?

Another type of general research is the accumulation of biographical information. Although this seems to be rather difficult for most students, it need not be. The steps of the procedure are somewhat different from the first outline.

1. Even if you know the general background of a person, begin with the general biographical sources, A5–A6, and those listed under subject fields. The most important general source of information is the *Biography Index*.
2. General sources will supply or verify basic data on your subject. The person's country or occupation can be important steppingstones to other information about him.
3. Check the bibliographies against the card catalog. Look for general works on the subject's country and occupation.
4. Although the *Biography Index* is most useful, it will be necessary to check all periodical indexes published prior to it.
5. Especially for criticism of an author, see references under literature: authors, works, criticisms of, B171.

6. Check other bibliographical sources for works not listed in general works. This may mean using interlibrary loans, so start your research early. The following outline summarizes this procedure.

WORKING OUTLINE II

This outline illustrates the steps in the search for biographical information.

PERSON (your subject)
    Biography under subject fields in KEY TO REFERENCE BOOKS.
    Biographical sources, A5—A6
        Occupation (gives subject area to pursue)
        Dates (yearbooks)
        Country
        Bibliography (basic sources)
            Library card catalog
                Specific person
                Works mentioned in bibliography
                His occupation or country
                General works
            Biography Index (often best to turn here first; usually no need to look in the individual book covered by this index)
            For criticism, See: B171
            Other bibliographical sources, B11, and under subject fields.

    Interlibrary loan.

    See: Evaluations of biography books in How Do I Evaluate Books?

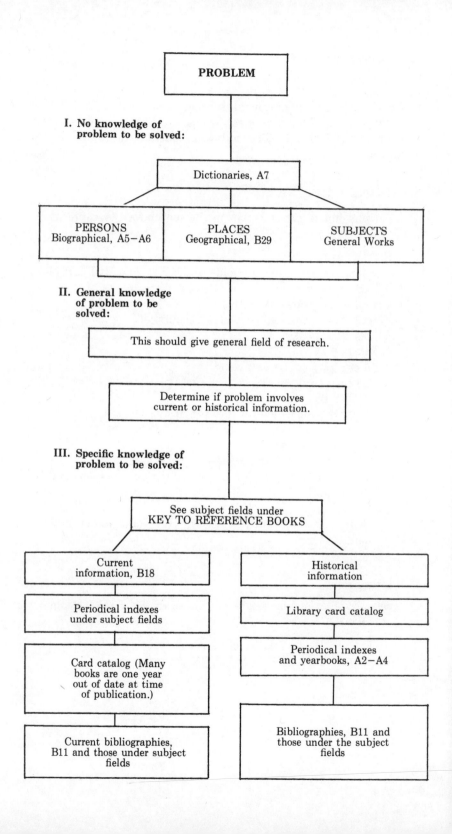

Often you can save time if you write down your problem and look for the key word or words. Table 1 contains examples of what to look for.

QUESTION (Key words to look for are set in italic type)	General Area in KEY TO REFERENCE BOOKS	Probable type of work to give answer
1. Where can I find the *poem*: "Runaway Boy"?	General information or Literature	Poems or poetry
2. *Newest* material on *teaching* reading?	Education	Indexes
3. What is the *address* of the American Jazz Association?	General information	Addresses — Associations
4. What *was* the *population* of the United States in 1899?	History	United States — statistics
5. Who *manufactures* Geritol?	Business	Manufactures
6. What does *RN* mean?	Dictionaries	Abbreviations
7. What is "Pennsylvania *Day*"?	General information	Holidays
8. Where do I find a *criticism* of an *author's* work?	Literature	Authors, works, criticisms of
9. Where can I find an interpretation of the *short story* . . . ?	Literature	Short stories — interpretation of
10. Which *religious denomination* is the United States is the *largest*?	Religion	Statistics
11. What are the *symptoms* of gout?	General information, Science, or Dictionaries	Medical dictionary

HOW DO I FIND SPECIFIC ANSWERS?

When given a problem for research, how do you proceed, especially if you do not understand the terminology or the subject matter of the problem? The sequence of steps in research for most problems is outlined below and graphically illustrated:

1. Use dictionaries to define unknown terminology.
   a. General dictionaries, B7
   b. Subject dictionaries listed under subject fields in KEY TO REFERENCE BOOKS
   c. If not found in one of these dictionaries, you may assume the term is too new to be listed in a dictionary and you should search under current information, B18.
2. From the definition, determine the general category the problem falls into: persons (biography), places (geography), or subjects. (See KEY TO REFERENCE BOOKS.)
3. Determine whether the problem involves current or historical information.
4. Turn to the most likely subject field under the KEY TO REFERENCE BOOKS. The works listed here are mainly stepping-stones to the solution, rather than the answer itself.
5. The types of reference works to look in are listed in the illustration in logical sequence of procedure (page 40).
6. Solution (we hope).
7. "Stumped"? Ask the reference librarian for help, and don't be afraid to ask a second time if you are not satisfied with the first answer.
8. See also: p.41.

HOW TO GET THE MOST HELP FROM REFERENCE LIBRARIANS

The primary purpose of a reference librarian is to assist you in using the library and locating sources. However, communicating your needs to a reference librarian may not be as easy as it would seem. The gap which is frequently encountered between student and librarian does not imply lack of intelligence on the part of either; both must attempt to bridge the gap. We are concerned here primarily with the student communicating his needs in a manner which enables him to be successful in as little time as possible. No one technique will always work, but the following points will prove valuable in communicating with a reference librarian.

BASIC

If your library publishes a guide to the use of the library—read it first.

HOW TO BEGIN

1. A little thought before asking for help may save considerable time.
2. What do you really need? Maybe you don't really know; maybe you're not exactly sure—a little confused?
3. If confused, tell the reference librarian. Don't pretend you know—it just doesn't help in the long run.
4. If you do understand what you need be sure to (at least once) say to yourself what you intend asking the reference librarian. Does it make sense the way you're saying it? Many feel that if you write down what you wish to ask, you can make your questions clear and intelligent.

HOW TO ASK–THE FOLLOWING SEQUENCE IS SUGGESTED

1. Give the reference librarian the purpose of your need.
   a. State the assignment, give the course or subject field, length of paper or speech and date due. This general information will start the cogs moving in a good reference librarian, and help him to focus on your need.
   b. Depth of paper. Your status as a student (freshman or graduate) tells the librarian more than you may imagine.
2. Be as specific as possible. This may not always be an easy task.
   a. Begin by stating your need or what you seek in the most specific manner possible. State clearly just what you want: statistics, criticism or general information and the amount you need, whether it's current, historical, or biographical.
   b. If you suspect the reference librarian misunderstands you, repeat your need or explain it further by broadening the scope of your subject. Remember, the reference librarian is not a walking encyclopedia, just one who has skill in pointing out the most likely sources to pursue.

    c. When you ask "who wrote", request an item by title . . . indicate that the title mentioned is a poem, a short story, a drama or admit uncertainty if you don't know.

3. Tell where you have looked, and briefly how you proceeded, the time you spent, what you looked under, what periodical indexes were used, and names of other reference books consulted. This may indicate to the reference librarian the extent of your knowledge of the subject and the direction in which he should proceed.

HOW TO LISTEN

Over-familiarity with library resources tends to cause reference librarians to assume a student's knowledge of the library is greater than it is. Because of this frequent, although unconscious, attitude on the part of the reference librarian, you should *always* ask for clarification of his answers whenever in doubt. Don't be afraid to show your ignorance. After all, reference librarians exist upon the assumption that students are not specialized in using a library. When he suggests you consult a source unfamiliar to you, ask for its location and how to use it. In the long run, the time saved will be more important to you than retaining your ego. Remember you are in the library to obtain information, not to show how much you know. So don't leave until you are completely satisfied that you've found all that is available there.

HOW TO "RE-ASK"

If the reference librarian sent you on a "wild goose chase", or up a "dead-end street", don't stop your search. Remember, the normal response of the reference librarian to any question is to send you to the most likely sources first. Rather than naming 15 possible sources, and confusing you, he will mention only 3 or 4 at the most. The very fact that you need to return to the reference librarian, (his first suggestions having failed to uncover anything or insufficient information) will become a challenge to any good librarian to locate the information if at all possible. If information is still lacking when time has run out for today, ask the reference librarian to keep your need in mind and tell him you will stop again the next day or so. He may just come up with what you need during this time. This is another reason you ought not to procrastinate—give the reference librarian a chance to help you. *Help the reference librarian to help you.*

KEY TO REFERENCE BOOKS

Basic General Reference Works

Knowledge of dictionaries, encyclopedias, yearbooks, periodical indexes, and biographical sources, is essential to research. The following examples are basic reference works for all fields.

They are as essential to the researcher as a pick and shovel are to a treasure hunter. All the following reference works, except the dictionaries, are indicated in chart form. The charts are so arranged that when you look for a general subject, "X" will correspond with the subject and the best reference works in this author's opinion. "XX" indicates first choice when more than one reference work is suggested.

To facilitate the finding of specific reference works, each subject has been assigned a code number. The code numbers are formed by giving a letter to each main section under KEY TO REFERENCE BOOKS: "A" to the Basic General Reference Works, and "B" to Basic Reference Works in Various Fields. The subject entries are numbered consecutively.

■ A1 ENCYCLOPEDIAS*

	Encyclopedia Americana (AE5.E333)	Encyclopaedia Britannica (AE5.E363)	Lincoln† Library (AG105.L55)	Columbia† Encyclopedia (AE5.C725)
Arrangement, alphabetical	X	X		X
Arrangement, topical			X	
Bibliographies	X	X		X
Biographies, past and present	X	X	X	X
Costume	XX	X		
Digest of books and opera	X			
Education, general articles	X	X	X	X
English language	X	X	X	
Historical subjects	X	XX	X	X
History of each century	X			
Literature	X	X	X	X
Long articles	Some	X		
Paintings of great masters, evaluation of	X			
Religions and Bible	X	X		X
Scientific subjects	XX	X	X	X
Short articles	X		X	X

*This list does not cover all subjects, only representative examples of similarities and differences.

†These are one and/or two volume sets.

■ **A2 THE FOUR MOST USEFUL YEARBOOKS***

	Information Please Almanac (AY64.I55)	World Almanac (AY67.N5W7)	Statistical Abstract of the United States (HA202.)	Stateman's Year-Book (JA51.S7)
Bibliography	X		X	X
Constitution of the United States	X	X		
Cost of living		X	X	
Education	X	X	X	X
Forms of address	XX	X		
Headline stories of the year	X			
International in scope	X	X	last chapter	XX
International organizations	X	X		XX
International tables, comparative				agricultural only
Inventions and discoveries	X	XX	X	
National in scope			X	
Parliamentary procedure	X			
Political and economic geography				XX
Postal regulations	X	X		
Religion	X	X	X	X
Sports	X	X		
Tables cover more than one year	X	X	XX	X
United States statistics in summary	X	XX	XX	X

*This list does not cover all subjects, only representative examples of similarities and differences.

■ A3 ENCYCLOPEDIA YEARBOOKS*

	Americana Annual (AE5.E333a)	Britannica Book of the Year (AE5.E364)
Colleges and universities, list of	X	
Cumulative index	covers four preceding years	covers four preceding years
List of major events in order of their occurrence	X	X
List of various happenings alphabetically organized	X	
Long articles		Some
Obituaries	Under heading "Necrology"	X
Photographs and illustrations	X	X
Societies and organizations, a selected list	X	X
Special calendar of major holidays and anniversaries of the year		X
Statistical data	X	X

*This list does not cover all subjects, only representative examples of similarities and differences.

■ A4 PERIODICAL INDEXES

	Applied Science and Technology Index	Education Index	Social Sciences Index	Humanities Index	The New York Times Index	Public Affairs Information Service	Readers' Guide*
Business					X		X
Economics			X		X	X	X
Education and psychology		X	X		X		X
Fine arts					X		X
History			X		X	X	X
Languages and literature				X			
Philosophy				X			
Physical education		X			X		X
Political science			X		X	X	X
Religion				X	X		X
Science and technology	X		Up to 1955		X	X	X
Sociology			X		X	X	

*Although the *Readers' Guide* is the most widely known of all the indexes, it is not always the best one to use or the first to which you should go. The other indexes are more specialized and thus give the best information in their fields.

■ A5 GENERAL WORLDWIDE BIOGRAPHICAL SOURCES* (SEE ALSO B11a)

	If little known about person, begin here	Brief treatment	Extensive treatment	Contemporary only	Past and present	Includes lesser known persons	Portraits	Published annually	List of sources to other information
Current Biography (CT100.C8)	X		X	X			X	X	X
General Encyclopedias (20 per cent or more biographies)	X	X	X		X	X	X	X	X
International Who's Who (CT120.I44)		X		X		X		X	
New Century Cyclopedia of Names (PE1625.C43)		X			X	X			
New York Times Index (Z1219.C95)		X		X	X	X		X	
Webster's Biographical Dictionary (CT103.W4)	X	X			X	X			

*The *Biography Index* is the best current guide to worldwide biographical sources. Both prominent and less important people will be found here, as will persons of both past and present. It covers most major periodicals (about 1500), books, portions of books, obituaries in periodicals, and selected ones from *The New York Times*. Portraits are indicated when they appear in conjunction with indexed material.

■ A6 GEOGRAPHICAL BIOGRAPHICAL SOURCES (SEE ALSO B11a and under Subjects)

	Living persons	Nonliving persons	Brief	Detailed	Bibliographies	Supplements	Portraits	Must use index	Facsimiles of autographs
AMERICAN									
Dictionary of American Biography (E176.D562)		X		X	X	X			
National Cyclopedia of American Biography (E176.N28)	X	X		X	X	X	X	X	
Who's Who in America (E663.W56)	X		X						
Who Was Who in America (E663.W54)		X	X						
Appleton's Cyclopedia of American Biography (E176.A666)		X		X		X	X		X
BRITISH									
Dictionary of National Biography* (DA28.D45)		X		X	X	X			
Who's Who (DA28.W6)	X		X						
Who Was Who (DA28.W65)		X	X						

*Many Americans of the Colonial period are included in the main set.

■A7 DICTIONARIES

1. Things to remember:
   a. Dictionaries may be very helpful when writing a research paper.
   b. No one dictionary will give you all the information available.
   c. There is no single correct pronunciation or proper meaning for every word.
   d. Many dictionaries also have special features, such as biographical names and a list of colleges and universities.
2. The four most commonly used unabridged dictionaries:
   a. FUNK & WAGNALLS NEW STANDARD DICTIONARY OF THE ENGLISH LANGUAGE, 1964, Funk & Wagnalls. (PE1625.S7)
   b. THE OXFORD ENGLISH DICTIONARY, 12 vols. and Suppls., 1933, Oxford. (Same as NEW ENGLISH DICTIONARY ON HISTORICAL PRINCIPLES.)
   c. WEBSTER'S NEW INTERNATIONAL DICTIONARY OF THE ENGLISH LANGUAGE, 2nd ed., 1950, Merriam-Webster. (PE1625.W3)
   d. WEBSTER'S THIRD NEW INTERNATIONAL DICTIONARY OF THE ENGLISH LANGUAGE, 1964, Merriam-Webster. (PE1625.W36)
3. Where can I find information about a specific word? The following are examples (not a complete list):

ABBREVIATIONS

ABBREVIATIONS: A REVERSE GUIDE, 1971, Pierian. (PE1693.R94)

ABBREVIATIONS DICTIONARY, 4th ed., 1974. American Elsevier. (PE1693.D4)

ABBREVIATIONS DICTIONARY, 1964, Duell, Sloan and Pearce. (PE1693.D4)

COMPLETE DICTIONARY OF ABBREVIATIONS, rev. ed., 1959, Crowell. (PE1693.S35)

CONCISE DICTIONARY OF ABBREVIATION, 1961, Tudor. (PE1693.M35)

WORLD GUIDE TO ABBREVIATIONS OF ASSOCIATIONS AND ORGANIZATIONS, 2 vols., 2nd ed., 1970–71, Bowker. (P365.S6)

See also: Most general dictionaries.

ACRONYMS
ACRONYMS AND INITIALISMS DICTIONARY, 4th ed. and
Suppl., 1974, Gale. (PE1693.G3)
REVERSE ACRONYMS AND INITIALISMS DICTIONARY,
1972, Gale. (PE1693.R4)

BRIEF DICTIONARY
AMERICAN COLLEGE DICTIONARY, 1966, Random.
(PE1628.A55)
FUNK & WAGNALLS STANDARD COLLEGE DICTIONARY,
1973, Funk & Wagnalls. (PE1628.S586)
WEBSTER'S NEW COLLEGIATE DICTIONARY, 8th ed., 1973,
Merriam. (PE1628.W4M4)

CODE NAMES
CODE NAMES DICTIONARY, 1963, Gale. (PE1693.R9)

FOREIGN WORD MEANINGS
See: B163—B167.

LEGAL TERMS
WORDS AND PHRASES, 88 Vols., 1940—, (Kept up to date by
cumulative annual parts), West. Very useful for all subjects.
(KF156.W6)

ORIGINS OF WORDS AND PHRASES
BREWER'S DICTIONARY OF PHRASE AND FABLE, 13th rev.
ed., 1972, Harper. (PN43.B65)
DICTIONARY OF WORD AND PHRASE ORIGINS, 1962,
Harper. (PE1580.M613)
DICTIONARY OF WORD ORIGINS, 1961, Littlefield.
(PE1580.S5)
OXFORD ENGLISH DICTIONARY, 12 Vols. and Suppls., Oxford.
(PE1625.M7)

PRONUNCIATION, THE BEST
THE AMERICAN PRONOUNCING DICTIONARY OF
TROUBLESOME WORDS, 1950, Crowell. (PE1137.C56)
DICTIONARY OF PRONUNCIATION, Rev. ed., 1971, A. S.
Barnes. (PE1137.N65)
NBC HANDBOOK OF PRONUNCIATION, 3rd ed., 1963,
Crowell. (PE1137.B573)

SLANG AND IDIOMS

THE AMERICAN THESAURUS OF SLANG, 2nd ed., 1953, Crowell. (PE3729.A5B4)

DICTIONARY OF AMERICAN SLANG, 2nd ed., 1967, Crowell. (PE3729.U5W4)

DICTIONARY OF AMERICAN UNDERWORLD LINGO, 1950, Twayne. (PE3726.D5)

DICTIONARY OF SLANG AND UNCONVENTIONAL ENGLISH, 7th ed., 1971, Macmillan. (PE3721.P3)

DICTIONARY OF THE UNDERWORLD, rev. ed., 1964, Routledge. (PE3726.P3)

NARCOTICS, LINGO, AND LORE, 1959, C. C. Thomas. (PE3727.N3S3)

SLANG AND ITS ANALOGUES, 1970, Arno. (PE3721.F4)

THE UNDERGROUND DICTIONARY: A GUIDE TO THE LANGUAGE OF THE AMERICAN DRUG CULTURE, 1971, Simon & Schuster. (PE3721.L3)

SYNONYMS AND ANTONYMS

CRABB'S ENGLISH SYNONYMS, rev. ed., 1917, Grosset and Dunlap. (PE1591.C7)

DICTIONARY OF ENGLISH SYNONYMS, rev. ed., 1959, Little. (PE1591.S7)

NEW ROGET'S THESAURUS OF THE ENGLISH LANGUAGE IN DICTIONARY FORM, rev. ed., 1961, Putnam. (PE1591.L43)

ROGET'S INTERNATIONAL THESAURUS, 3rd ed., 1962, Crowell. (PE1591.M37)

WEBSTER'S DICTIONARY OF SYNONYMS, 2nd ed., 1968, Merriam. (PE1591.W4)

WORDS OF AMERICAN ORIGIN AND USAGES

A DICTIONARY OF AMERICAN ENGLISH ON HISTORICAL PRINCIPLES, 4 vols., 2nd ed., 1960, University of Chicago. (PE2835.C72)

A DICTIONARY OF AMERICANISMS ON HISTORICAL PRINCIPLES, 1956, University of Chicago. (PE2835.D5)

WORDS THAT RHYME

NEW RHYMING DICTIONARY AND POET'S HANDBOOK, 1957, Harper. (PE1519.J6)

WOOD'S UNABRIDGED RHYMING DICTIONARY, 1943, World. (PE1519.W62)

Basic Reference Works in Various Fields

Reference books contain time-saving compilations of facts. Reference works are known primarily by their titles, and are so listed. The following sections are listed by general subject fields alphabetically following General Information. The field of General Information covers almost everything—mainly information students frequently ask about or look for in the library, not directly connected with a given course. The following subject fields will supplement courses, serve as stepping-off places for work on a research paper, or supply specific answers to problems.

The value of general reference works is seldom realized. The researcher may save many an hour and much frustration by glancing through the appropriate section here, looking for likely works, and then proceeding.

Each reference work is followed by the number of volumes (if there are more than one), the edition, publishing date, and publisher. A brief note indicating its value or content follows each title unless the name of the title and/or subject heading is self-evident. Most college and university libraries use the Library of

Congress Classification for arrangement of their books on the
shelves. (See examples in the Appendix.) The Library of Congress
Classification number is given for each title. Periodical Indexes are
normally arranged alphabetically by title at a given location in the
library.

If your library uses the Dewey Decimal System, simply consult
the library card catalog under the title will give you the location of
each volume in your library. Cross references (**See** and **See also**)
refer to the correct listing or additional information by code number
rather than by page.

B8–B50 GENERAL INFORMATION

ABBREVIATIONS
See: A7

■ **B8 ADDRESS OF:**

COLLEGES
EDUCATION DIRECTORY, part 3, 1912–, U.S. Government
   Printing Office. (L111.A6)
See also: B15.

COLLEGES OVERSEAS
INTERNATIONAL HANDBOOK OF UNIVERSITIES, 4th ed.,
   1971, American Council on Education. (L900.I58)
STUDY ABROAD, (Annual), Unipub. (LB2338.S86)
WORLD LIST, (every two years) International Association of
   Universities. (L900.I57)
THE WORLD OF LEARNING, 1947– (annual), Gale. (AS2.W6)

CONGRESSMEN
CONGRESSIONAL STAFF DIRECTORY, (Annual)
   Congressional Staff Directory. Biographies, phone nos., ad-
   dresses. (JK1012.C65)
OFFICIAL CONGRESSIONAL DIRECTORY (Irregular), 1809–,
   U.S. Government Printing Office. (JK1011.U52)

FACULTY
THE NATIONAL FACULTY DIRECTORY, 2 vols., (Annual)
   Gale. (L901.N34)

FOUNDATIONS
FOUNDATION DIRECTORY, 5th ed., 1975, Russell Sage. (AS911.A2F65)
GRANTS REGISTER 1974–75, 1974, St. Martin. (LB2338.G631)

GOVERNMENT
UNITED STATES GOVERNMENT ORGANIZATION MANUAL, 1935–, U.S. Government Printing Office. (JK421.A3)

MANUFACTURES
THOMAS REGISTER OF AMERICAN MANUFACTURES, 1905-, (annual), Thomas. (E302.J4632)

ORGANIZATIONS
ENCYCLOPEDIA OF ASSOCIATIONS, (annual), Gale. (HS17.G33)
U.S. GOVERNMENT ORGANIZATIONAL MANUAL (annual), U.S. Government Printing Office. (HS17.G33)
YEARBOOK OF INTERNATIONAL ORGANIZATIONS (annual), International Pub. (JX1904.A42)
See also: A2, B21 and under subject fields.

PEOPLE
Telephone books.
"Who's Who" books.
See also: A5–A6.

PERIODICALS AND NEWSPAPERS
AYER'S DIRECTORY OF NEWSPAPERS AND PERIODICALS, 1880– , (annual), Ayer. (Z6951.A97)
ULRICH'S PERIODICAL DIRECTORY, 2 vols., 15th ed., 1973, Bowker. About 50,000 listed (Z6941.U5)

PUBLISHERS
AMERICAN BOOK TRADE DIRECTORY, revised frequently, Bowker. Also lists dealers in foreign books, and so forth. (Z475.A5)
LITERARY MARKET PLACE, 1940– (annual). Bowker. Best for United States publishers. (PN161.L5)
See also:B13.

PUBLISHERS, FOREIGN
PUBLISHERS' INTERNATIONAL DIRECTORY, 1972, Bowker, (Z282.P73)

PUBLISHERS INTERNATIONAL YEAR BOOK: WORLD DIRECTORY (annual). London, Wales. (Z282.P8)

■ B9 AUDIO-VISUAL AIDS

EDUCATIONAL MEDIA YEARBOOK, 1973– , Bowker. Comprehensive in coverage. (LB1028.3.E37)

EDUCATORS GUIDE TO FREE FILMSTRIPS (annual). Educators Progress Service. (LB1044.E3)

EDUCATORS GUIDE TO FREE TAPES, SCRIPTS, AND TRANSCRIPTIONS (annual) Educators Progress Service. (LB1044.2.E3)

INDEX TO EDUCATIONAL AUDIO TAPES, 2nd ed., 1972, U. of S. California. (LB1044.4.Z9N3)

INDEX TO EDUCATIONAL OVERHEAD TRANSPARENCIES, 3rd ed., 1973, U. of S. California. (LB1044.9.Z9)

INDEX TO EDUCATIONAL RECORDS, 2nd ed., 1972, U. of S. California. Range is from pre-school through adult education plus special uses. (LB1044.3.Z933)

INDEX TO EDUCATIONAL VIDEOTAPES, 2nd ed., 1973 U. of S. California. (LB1044.7.Z9N3)

INDEX TO 8MM EDUCATIONAL MOTION CARTRIDGES, 3rd ed., 1973 U. of S. California. (LB1044.Z9)

INDEX TO HEALTH AND SAFETY EDUCATION (MULTIMEDIA), 1972, U. of S. California. (LC1044.N3)

INDEX TO PSYCHOLOGY: MULTIMEDIA, 1972, U. of S. California. Range is from pre-school to adult, plus special uses. (BF77.N37)

INDEX TO 16MM EDUCATIONAL FILMS, 3 vols., 4th ed., 1973 U. of S. California. (Z5814.M8N35)

INDEX TO 35MM EDUCATIONAL FILMSTRIPS, 4th ed., 1973, U. of S. California. (Z5814.M8N36)

INDEX TO VOCATIONAL TECHNICAL EDUCATION (MULTIMEDIA), 1972, U. of S. California. (LB1044.Z9N36)

NICEM UPDATE OF NONBOOK MEDIA, 1973– (monthly), U. of S. California. A monthly subscription service records new media items up-dating the 14 NICEM indexes. (LB1043. Z9N32)

See also: B109, B133.

AUTHORS
See: B171.

■B10 AWARDS

AWARDS, HONORS AND PRIZES, 3rd ed., 1975, Gale. Provides essential facts about awards for notable achievements in various fields. 7th ed., 1970. (AS8.W38)

THE BLUE BOOK OF AWARDS, 1956, Marquis. Lists major prizes, medals, honors, and distinctions and information about each. (AS8.B7)

HANDBOOK OF SCIENTIFIC AND TECHNICAL AWARDS IN THE U.S. AND CANADA, 1900–1952, 1956, Special Library Association. Covers most fields of science and technology between 1900–1952. (Q141.S63)

HISTORY OF THE NEWBERY AND CALDECOTT MEDALS, 1957, Viking. Covers annual awards for children's books. Lists winners. (Z1037.S648)

LITERARY AND LIBRARY PRIZES, 1970, Bowker. Lists winners, prize contests, and fellowships. (PN171.P75L5)

NOBEL: THE MAN AND HIS PRIZES, 1901–1962, 7th ed., 1970, American Elsevier. Biography of Nobel, listing of prize winners. (PN171.P75L5)

THE PULITZER PRIZE STORY, 1974, Columbia. Covers outstanding achievements in American journalism. (PS647.N4H6)

■B11 BIBLIOGRAPHY, GENERAL (GOOD FOR MOST SUBJECTS)

AMERICAN BOOK PUBLISHING RECORD, 1960– (monthly and annually), Bowker. Covers all books published in the United States by author, title, and subject for the previous month. (Z1201.A52)

AMERICAN REFERENCE BOOKS ANNUAL, 1970– (annual), Libraries Unlimited. Reviews reference books published during that year. (Z1035.1.A55)

THE BIBLIOGRAPHICAL INDEX, 1937– (by subject), Wilson. Current bibliographies in books, pamphlets, and periodicals. (Z1002.B594)

CUMULATIVE BOOK INDEX, 1928–date, Wilson. (It supplements the U.S. CATALOG, which lists all books in print on January 1, 1928). Lists books in English by author, title, and subject. (Z1215.U6)

A GUIDE TO THE STUDY OF THE UNITED STATES OF AMERICA, 1960. U.S. Government Printing Office (by subject). Representative books reflecting the development of American life and thought. Annotated. (Z1215.U53)

GUIDE TO U.S. GOVERNMENT PUBLICATIONS, 3 vols., 1973. Documents Index. A looseleaf service keeps information up-to-date. Covers serials, periodicals, and monographs. Annotated. (Z1223.Z7A5722)

NATIONAL UNION CATALOG (books representing the holdings of the Library of Congress, by author and by subject since 1950). (Z881.U49A212)

PUBLISHER'S WEEKLY, 1872– (weekly), Bowker. List of books published by author; some have notes about the book's contents.

A WORLD BIBLIOGRAPHY OF BIBLIOGRAPHIES. Besterman, Theodore, 4th ed., 5 vols., 1965–69, Lausanne, Societas. Most comprehensive guide available; listed by subject. (Z1002. B5685)

See also: The library card catalog; and B13, B50a.

▪B11a BIOGRAPHY

BIOGRAPHICAL DICTIONARIES AND RELATED WORKS: A BIBLIOGRAPHY, 1967, Gale. Covers 19th and 20th century publications. Includes a comprehensive index. (Z5301.S55)

CHAMBER'S BIOGRAPHICAL DICTIONARY, 1969, St. Martin's. (CT103.C4)

MODERN ENGLISH BIOGRAPHY, by Frederic Boase, 1965, Frank Cass & Co. 30,000 sketches of persons who died between 1851–1900 (CT1773.B6)

THE NEW YORK TIMES BIOGRAPHICAL EDITION, 1971– (weekly), The New York Times. Current profiles cumulatively indexed every week for six months. Includes everyone who makes news. (CT120.N45)

NEW YORK TIMES OBITUARIES INDEX, 1969, New York Times. Over 350,000 death listings from 1858–1968. (CT213.N47)

NOTABLE AMERICAN WOMEN, 1607 – 1850, A BIOGRAPHICAL DICTIONARY, 3 vols., 1971, Harvard. (CT3260.N57)

WHO'S WHO IN THE EAST, Marquis Who's Who, Inc. (E176. W643)

WHO'S WHO IN THE MIDWEST, Marquis Who's Who, Inc. (E176.W644)

WHO'S WHO IN THE SOUTH AND SOUTHWEST, Marquis Who's Who, Inc. (F208.W64)

WHO'S WHO IN THE WEST, Marquis Who's Who, Inc. (F595.W64)

See also: A5–A6 and biography, under subject fields (B51–B264)

■B12 BOOK REVIEWS

BOOK REVIEW DIGEST, 1905– , Wilson. Indexes reviews of current books from about seventy periodicals. (Z1219.C95)

BOOK REVIEW INDEX, 1965– (annual). Gale. Comprehensive. (Z1219.B65)

INDEX TO BOOK REVIEWS IN THE HUMANITIES, 1960– (annual), P. Thomson. Little duplication between this and BOOK REVIEW DIGEST. (Z1035.A1I63)

A GUIDE TO BOOK REVIEW CITATIONS: A BIBLIOGRAPHY OF SOURCES, 1969, Ohio State. (Z1035.A1G7)

MASTERPLOTS (annual), Salem. (Also a number of series issued frequently.) Summary of plot and action of novels, plays, poems, and short stories. (PN44.M33A5)

TECHNICAL BOOK REVIEW INDEX, 1917– (monthly), Special Libraries Association. Much like the BOOK REVIEW DIGEST, but for technical books. (Z7913.T36)

THESAURUS OF BOOK DIGESTS, 1944, Crown. Synopsis of best literary works. (PN44.H38)

T. L. S. . . . ESSAYS AND REVIEWS FROM THE TIMES LITERARY SUPPLEMENT, 1963– (annual), Oxford. Critical record of the most important books in many fields. (PN501.T22)

See also: The annual index of a periodical; they usually list all books that they have reviewed. See current periodicals and newspapers in the particular field desired; also B171.

■B13 BOOKS IN PRINT

BOOKS IN PRINT, 1948– (annual), Bowker. Listed by author and title including all U.S. books currently in print. (Z1215.P97)

BRITISH BOOKS IN PRINT (annual), Bowker. (Z2001.R33)

CATALOG OF REPRINTS IN SERIES (frequently revised), Scarecrow. Gives reprint editions of certain works now available. (Z1033.S5C3)

MONTHLY CATALOG OF U.S. GOVERNMENT PUBLICATIONS (monthly). U.S. Government Printing Office. All publications issued by government bodies.

PAPERBOUND BOOKS IN PRINT (annual), Bowker. Listed by author, title, and subject. (Z1215.P105)

PUBLISHER'S TRADE LIST ANNUAL (annual), Bowker. Compilation of publishers' catalogs. (Z1215.P97)

SUBJECT GUIDE TO BOOKS IN PRINT (annual), Bowker. List of books in print by subject. (Z1215.P973)

TEXTBOOKS IN PRINT, 1926– , Bowker. Covers elementary through high school books and some professional books for teachers. (Z581.A51)

WHITAKER'S REFERENCE CATALOGUE TO CURRENT LITERATURE, 2 vols. (British publications, intermittent), Whitaker. By author and title. (Z2005.W57)

■ B13a CAMPS

GUIDE TO SUMMER CAMPS AND SUMMER SCHOOLS (annual), Sergent. (GV193.G8)

See also: B21.

■ B14 COLLEGE COLORS

OUR COLLEGE COLORS, 1949, Kutztown Publications. (LB3630.S6)

■ B15 COLLEGES, INFORMATION ABOUT

AMERICAN JUNIOR COLLEGES, 8th ed., 1971, American Council on Education. Accredited two-year institutions. (L901.A53)

COMPARATIVE GUIDE TO JUNIOR AND TWO-YEAR COMMUNITY COLLEGES, 1972, Harper. (LB2328.C355)

AMERICAN UNIVERSITIES AND COLLEGES, 1973 (revised frequently), American Council on Education. Accredited colleges and universities in the United States. (LA226.A65)

COMMONWEALTH UNIVERSITIES YEARBOOK, 1914– (annual), Association of Commonwealth Universities. Arranged by country. (LB2310.Y5)

COUNSELORS' COMPARATIVE GUIDE TO AMERICAN COLLEGES, 1974, Harper. (L901.C33)

EDUCATION DIRECTORY, part 3, 1912– (annual). U.S. Government Printing Office. (L111.A6)

INTERNATIONAL HANDBOOK OF UNIVERSITIES, 4th ed., 1971, International Association of Universities. Details covering admission requirements, fees, and such. (L900.I58)

LOVEJOY'S COLLEGE GUIDE, 1940– (annual), Simon and Schuster. Listed by state. Gives basic data plus student-faculty ratio. (LA226.L6)

PATTERSON'S AMERICAN EDUCATION, 1904– (annual), Educational Directories, Inc. Classified directory of schools, and educational systems of the states and their officers. (L901.P3)

See also: B30, B47, and individual college catalogs.

∎B16 COLLEGE PUBLICATIONS

AYER'S DIRECTORY OF NEWSPAPERS AND PERIODICALS, 1880– (annual), Ayer. (Z6951.A97)

∎B17 COPYRIGHT INFORMATION

A COPYRIGHT GUIDE, 2nd ed., 1963, Bowker. (KF2986.P45)

A MANUAL OF COPYRIGHT PRACTICE, by Margaret Nicholson, 2nd ed., 1956, Oxford. (KF2994.N5)

CRITICISMS OF AUTHORS

See: B12, B171.

∎B18 CURRENT INFORMATION

CONGRESSIONAL QUARTERLY ALMANAC, 1945– (annual and weekly), Congressional Quarterly. Presents facts on Congress and politics. Complete, concise, unbiased. (JK1.C66)

FACTS ON FILE, 1941– (annual and weekly), Facts on File, Inc. (D410.F3)

KEESING'S CONTEMPORARY ARCHIVES, WEEKLY DIARY OF WORLD EVENTS WITH INDEX CONTINUALLY KEPT UP-TO-DATE, 1931– (weekly), Keesing's (D410.K4)

THE NEW YORK TIMES INDEX, 1851–, The New York Times. (AI21.N44)

News Letters . . . See: B37.

Periodicals and newspapers, See: A4 and KEY TO PERIODICALS for current periodicals.

Yearbooks . . . See: A2–A3, also consult periodical indexes.

▪B19 DATES

BOOK OF DAYS, 2 vols., 1899, W. and R. Chambers (Reprinted 1967) Gale. Arranged by day of year, emphasis on United Kingdom. (DA110.C52)

CELEBRATIONS: THE COMPLETE BOOK OF AMERICAN HOLIDAYS, 1972, Doubleday. Arranged chronologically from New Year's to Christmas. (GT4803.A2M84)

DICTIONARY OF DATES, by J. Haydn, 25th ed., 1911, Putnam. By subject up to 1910. (D9.H45)

DICTIONARY OF DATES, by H. R. Keller, 1934, Macmillan. Events to 1930 by country. (D9.K4)

EVERYONE'S DICTIONARY OF DATES, 1954, Dutton. Events to 1953. (D9.D5)

HISTORICAL TABLES, 58 B.C.–A.D. 1963, 1964, St. Martin's. Tabular chronology of world history arranged by periods. (D11.S83)

INSTANT ALMANAC OF EVENTS, ANNIVERSARIES, OBSERVANCES, QUOTATIONS, AND BIRTHDAYS FOR EVERY DAY OF THE YEAR, 1972, Parker. (D11.5.S66)

WHAT HAPPENED WHEN, 1966, Washburn. (D11.5.M57)

See also: A2–A3, B31.

▪B20 DEGREES

THE DEGREES AND HOODS OF THE WORLD'S UNIVERSITIES AND COLLEGES, 1948, Chestnut Press. (LB2389.H3)

See also: A7.

DIALOGS

See: B125.

▪B21 DIRECTORIES

DIRECTORIES OF GOVERNMENT AGENCIES, 1969, Libraries Unlimited. Very Comprehensive. (JK423.W9)

GUIDE TO AMERICAN DIRECTORIES, 9th ed., 1974, Klein. (Z5771.G8)

GUIDE TO AMERICAN EDUCATIONAL DIRECTORIES, 3rd ed., 1969, McGraw-Hill. (Z5813.G8)

See also: B8

■B22 DISSERTATIONS

COMPREHENSIVE DISSERTATION INDEX, 1861-1972, 37 vols., 1973, Xerox. Those accepted by U.S. academic institutions. Grouped by disciplines. Also an author index. (Z5055.U49C57)

GUIDE TO THESES AND DISSERTATIONS: AN INTERNATIONAL BIBLIOGRAPHY OF BIBLIO- GRAPHIES, 1975, Gale. (See Card Catalog)

DISSERTATION ABSTRACTS, 1938– (formerly called MICROFILM ABSTRACTS), University Microfilms. (Z5055.U5D64)

DOCTORAL DISSERTATIONS ACCEPTED BY AMERICAN UNIVERSITIES, 1934–1955 (annual), Wilson. Continued by DISSERTATION ABSTRACTS. (Z5055.U5D6)

■B22a DOCUMENTATION—RESEARCH PAPERS

A COMPLETE GUIDE TO ORGANIZING AND DOCUMENTING RESEARCH PAPERS. by G. W. Morse, 1974, Fleet. (LB2369.M6)

FORM AND STYLE IN THESIS WRITING, by W. G. Campbell, 4th ed., 1974, Houghton. (LB2369.C3)

A MANUAL FOR WRITERS OF TERM PAPERS, THESES, AND DISSERTATIONS, by K. L. Turobian, 4th ed., 1973, Univ. of Chicago. (LB2369.T8)

DRAMA

See: B138, B180

■B23 EMPLOYMENT

COLLEGE PLACEMENT ANNUAL (annual), The College Place- ment Council, Inc. (HF5382.5.U5C6)

THE DIRECTORY OF OVERSEAS SUMMER JOBS, (annual), National Directory Service. (HD6270.D5)

DIRECTORY OF SUMMER EMPLOYERS IN THE U.S., 1961, National Directory Service. (HF5382.5.U5D5)

EQUAL EMPLOYMENT OPPORTUNITY FOR MINORITY GROUP COLLEGE GRADUATES, 1972, Garrett Park. Com- prehensive guide to equal employment opportunity. (HF5549.5.M5C35)

LOOKING FOR EMPLOYMENT IN FOREIGN COUNTRIES: REFERENCE HANDBOOK, 6th ed., 1972, World Trade Academy. (HF5381.A7847)

NATIONAL DIRECTORY OF EMPLOYMENT SERVICES, 1962, Gale. Lists private, educational, and association employment services. (HD5873.N27)

THE PROFESSIONAL JOB CHANGING SYSTEM: WORLD'S FASTEST WAY TO GET A BETTER JOB, 3rd ed., 1974, Performance Dynamics. Covers strategy, associations, tests, interview techniques, and resumes. (HF5383.J28)

SUMMER EMPLOYMENT DIRECTORY OF THE UNITED STATES, (annual), National Directory Service. (HF5382.5.U5)

WORLD-WIDE SUMMER PLACEMENT DIRECTORY, 1952– (annual), The Advancement and Placement Institution. (HF5382.W6)

See also: B49.

■ **B24 ESSAYS**

ESSAY AND GENERAL LITERATURE INDEX, 1900–, Wilson. (AI3.E752)

■ **B25 ETIQUETTE**

ETIQUETTE, by E. Post, 12th ed., 1969, Funk. (BJ1853.P6)

NEW COMPLETE BOOK OF ETIQUETTE, by A. Vanderbilt, 1963, Doubleday. (BJ1853.V27)

NEW SEVENTEEN BOOK OF ETIQUETTE AND YOUNG LIVING, 1971, McKay. (BJ1857.C5H257)

FELLOWSHIPS

See: B45.

FILMS

See: B9

FINANCIAL AID

See: B45

■ **B26 FIRST FACTS**

FAMOUS FIRST FACTS, 3rd enlarged ed., 1963, Wilson. Events, discoveries, and inventions in the United States. Good indexes. (AG5.K315)

■B27 FRATERNITIES, SORORITIES, AND HONOR SOCIETIES

BAIRDS' MANUAL OF AMERICAN COLLEGE FRATERNITIES, 1963, George Banta. (LJ31.B2) See also: B21.

■B28 GARDENING

ENCYCLOPEDIA OF GARDENING, HORTICULTURE, AND LANDSCAPE DESIGN, 1961, Houghton. (SB45.T3)

■B28a GENERAL INFORMATION

CHAMBERS'S ENCYCLOPAEDIA, 4th ed., 15 vols. 1973, Pergamon Press. British emphasis. (AE5.C443)
COLLIER'S ENCYCLOPEDIA, Collier-Macmillian. (AE5.C683)
See also: A1−A3.

■B29 GEOGRAPHICAL INFORMATION

COLUMBIA-LIPPINCOTT GAZETTEER OF THE WORLD, 1952, Supplement 1962, Columbia University. Gives basic data on most all geographic place names in the world. (G103.L7)
DICTIONARY OF ALTITUDES IN THE UNITED STATES, 1906, Gale. (GB494.G3)
THE TIMES INDEX-GAZETTEER OF THE WORLD, 1965, Houghton. 343,000 geographical locations with coordinates of latitude and longitude. A cumulative index to THE TIMES ATLAS, but useful to all atlases. (G103.T5)
WEBSTER'S NEW GEOGRAPHICAL DICTIONARY, 1972, Merriam. Basic data on place names. (G103.W45)
See also: A1, B140. For new names of places, look in references listed under current information: B18.

GOVERNMENT PUBLICATIONS

See: B50

■B30 GRADUATE STUDY

ANNUAL GUIDES TO GRADUATE STUDY, 8 books, 1968− (annual, Peterson's Guides. Most comprehensive source on the U.S. (L901.P46)
GUIDE TO GRADUATE STUDIES IN GREAT BRITIAN, 1974, APS. Covers all subject areas. (LA637.T64)

A GUIDE TO GRADUATE STUDY, 4th ed., 1969, American
Council of Education. Lists information and requirements of
universities offering programs leading to the Ph.D. degree.
(LB2371.A4)
THE RANDOM HOUSE GUIDE TO GRADUATE STUDY IN
THE ARTS AND SCIENCES, 1967, Random. (LB2371.W36)
See also: individual college catalogs.

■B31 HOLIDAYS AND FESTIVALS

THE AMERICAN BOOK OF DAYS, 1948, Wilson. History, origin,
and customary observances. Also includes birthdays of famous
Americans. (GI4803.D6)
THE BOOK OF DAYS, 2 vols., 1899, W. and R. Chambers
(Reprinted 1967) Gale. By day of year, emphasis on United
Kingdom. Excellent. (DA110.C52)
THE BOOK OF FESTIVALS AND HOLIDAYS THE WORLD
OVER, 1970, Dodd. International in scope. Covers only
current ones. (GT3932.I27)
CELEBRATIONS: THE COMPLETE BOOK OF AMERICAN
HOLIDAYS, 1972, Doubleday. (GT4803.A2M84)
See also: A3, B19.

■B31a LIBRARIES—LOCATION

AMERICAN LIBRARY DIRECTORY, (annual), Bowker.
(Z731.A53)
DIRECTORY OF SPECIAL LIBRARIES AND INFORMATION
CENTERS, 3rd ed., 3 vols., 1974, Gale. Covers over 14,000
U.S. and Canadian special libraries, information centers, and
documentation centers. (Z731.K7)
SUBJECT COLLECTIONS: A GUIDE TO SPECIAL
LIBRARIES, 4th ed., 1974, Bowker. (Z688.A2A8)
WORLD GUIDE TO LIBRARIES, 4th ed., 2 vols., 1974, Bowker.
(Z721.I63)

■B32 LOCAL INFORMATION

City Directories (usually annual).
Newspapers.
Public libraries.
Court house or City Hall.
State Historical Society

MAPS

See: A1, B140

■B33 MEDICAL DICTIONARY

CYCLOPEDIC MEDICAL DICTIONARY, by Taber, 12th ed., 1973 (revised frequently), Davis. Not merely definitons, but additional information in the various fields of medical practice, nursing, and allied subjects. (R121.T18)

■B34 MICROFILMS

SUBJECT GUIDE TO MICROFILM IN PRINT, 1966– (biennial), Microcard Eds. (Z1033.M5S8)

UNION LIST OF MICROFILMS, 2 vols., 1961, Edwards. (Z1033.M5P5)

MONOLOGS

See: B125

■B35 MUSEUMS

DIRECTORY OF WORLD MUSEUMS, 1974, Columbia. List 22,000 museums and art galleries in 155 countries. (See Card Catalog)

THE OFFICIAL MUSEUM DIRECTORY, 1970, American Associated Museums. Covers U. S. and Canada. (AM10.A204)

■B35a NAMES

AMERICAN PLACE-NAMES: A CONCISE AND SELECTIVE DICTIONARY FOR THE CONTINENTAL UNITED STATES OF AMERICA, 1970, Oxford. Brief notes on origin and derivation. (E155.S79)

AMERICAN SURNAMES, 1969, Chilton. Covers meaning, derivation, nationality and frequency of type of family name born in the U.S. (CS2485.S63)

WEBSTER'S DICTIONARY OF PROPER NAMES, 1971, Merriam-Webster. Names unique to America, organized by subject. (PE1660.P34)

■B36 NEWS IN SUMMARY FORM

FACTS ON FILE, 1941– (annual and weekly), Facts of File, Inc. (D410.F3)

KEESING'S CONTEMPORARY ARCHIVES, WEEKLY DIARY
OF WORLD EVENTS WITH INDEX CONTINUALLY
KEPT UP-TO-DATE, 1931– (weekly), Keesing's (D410.K4)
See also: A4.

■ **B37 NEWSLETTERS**

NATIONAL DIRECTORY OF NEWSLETTERS AND
REPORTING SERVICE, 1966, Gale. (Z6941.N3)

■ **B38 NEWSPAPERS ON MICROFILM**

NEWSPAPERS IN MICROFILM: U.S., 1948– (Z6951.U469);
FOREIGN COUNTRIES, 1948– (Z6951.U515), Library of
Congress.

■ **B39 OCCUPATIONAL INFORMATION**

OCCUPATIONAL LITERATURE, 1971, Wilson (Z7164.V64F67)
OCCUPATIONAL OUTLOOK HANDBOOK (annual), U.S.
Government Printing Office (HD8051.A62)
See also: Library pamphlet file.

PAPERBOUND BOOKS

See: B13.

■ **B40 PHOTOGRAPHY—BIBLIOGRAPHY**

PHOTOGRAPHIC LITERATURE, 1963, Bowker. Covers books,
periodicals, and such. (Z7134.B6)

■ **B40a PICTURES**

PICTURE SOURCES, 3rd ed., 1973, Special Libraries Association.
By subject; addresses and telephone numbers are given.
(N4000.S7)
See Also: B122, B132.

PLACEMENT

See: B23, B77.

PLACES

See: B29.

PLAYS

See: B180.

■B41 POEMS

GRANGER'S INDEX TO POETRY, 6th ed., 1973, Columbia. By first line, author, and subject. (PN1021.G7)
POET'S HANDBOOK, 1969, Young. Places to send poems for publication. (PN161.H6)
See also: B191.

■B41a PORTRAITS

CYCLOPEDIA OF PORTRAITS, 10 vols., 1975, Gale. International. (See Card Catalog)
DICTIONARY OF AMERICAN PORTRAITS, 4045 PICTURES OF IMPORTANT AMERICANS FROM EARLIEST TIMES TO THE BEGINNING OF THE TWENTIETH CENTURY, 1967, Dover. (N7593.C53)

■B42 POST OFFICES

DIRECTORY OF POST OFFICES (annual), U.S. Government Printing Office. (HE6361.A312)

■B43 PUBLISHING A BOOK OR AN ARTICLE

A MANUAL OF STYLE, 12th ed., 1969, University of Chicago. The "how to" book of preparing works for publishing. (Z253.C57)
UNITED STATES GOVERNMENT PRINTING OFFICE STYLE MANUAL, rev. ed., 1967, U.S. Govt. Printing Office. (Z253. U58)
WRITER'S HANDBOOK, 1973, Writer. Sections on writing and commercial phases of authorship. (PN137.W73)
WRITER'S MARKET, 1930– (annual), Writer's Digest. Classifies list of markets for literary works. (PN161.W83)

■B44 QUOTATIONS

FAMILIAR QUOTATIONS, by J. Bartlett, 14th ed., 1968, Little. Most famous guide. Arranged chronologically by author with a comprehensive index. (PN6081.B27)
THE HOME BOOK OF QUOTATIONS, by B. Stevenson, 10th ed., 1967, Dodd. By subject. (PN6081.S73)
HOYT'S NEW CYCLOPEDIA OF PRACTICAL QUOTATIONS, 3rd ed., 1940, Funk. By subject. (PN6081.H7)
THE INTERNATIONAL THESAURUS OF QUOTATIONS, 1970, Crowell. A how-to-use quotations book. (PN6081.T77)

MACMILLAN BOOK OF PROVERBS, MAXIMS, AND FAMILIAR PHRASES, 1948, Macmillan. Very useful. (PN6405.S8)

MAGILL'S QUOTATIONS IN CONTEXT, 2 vols., 1965, Salem. (PN6081.M29)

THE OXFORD DICTIONARY OF ENGLISH PROVERBS, 3rd ed., 1971, Oxford. Alphabetical. (PN6421.09)

THE OXFORD DICTIONARY OF QUOTATIONS, 2nd ed., 1953, Oxford. (PN6081.09)

PROVERBS, SENTENCES AND PROVERBIAL PHRASES FROM ENGLISH WRITINGS MAINLY BEFORE 1500, 1968, Belknap. (PN6083.W45)

REPORT WRITING

See: B22a

■ **B45 SCHOLARSHIPS AND FELLOWSHIPS**

FELLOWSHIPS IN THE ARTS AND SCIENCES (annual), American Council on Education. (LB2371.A4)

A GUIDE TO FEDERAL ASSISTANCE FOR EDUCATION, 2 vols., 1972− (annual), Appleton. Looseleaf service, updated monthly. Most comprehensive guide on this subject. (LB2825.H6)

GRANTS AND AID TO INDIVIDUALS IN THE ARTS, 1972, Washington International Arts Letter (NX398.G7)

GRANTS REGISTER 1973−75, 1974, St. Martin. (LB2338.G631)

A NATIONAL CATALOG OF FINANCIAL AIDS FOR STUDENTS ENTERING COLLEGE, 6th ed., 1974, W.C. Brown. (LB2338.K4)

YOU CAN WIN A SCHOLARSHIP, 4th ed., 1972, Barron's. (LB2338.B76)

NATIONAL REGISTER OF SCHOLARSHIPS AND FELLOWSHIPS, 2 vols., 4th ed. (revised frequently), World Trade Academy. (LB2848.N3)

See also: College catalogs, B21, B47, and B8, Foundations.

SHORT STORIES

See: B194.

■ **B45a SKITS AND STUNTS**

INDEX TO SKITS AND STUNTS, 1958, Faxon. (Z5781.I7)

■B46 STATISTICS

A DICTIONARY OF STATISTICAL TERMS, 3rd ed., 1971, Hagner. (HA17.K4)

GUIDE TO U.S. GOVERNMENT STATISTICS, 3rd ed., 1961, Documents Index. A comprehensive guide by subject. (Z7554.U5G8)

STATISTICS SOURCES, 4th ed., 1974, Gale. Designed to identify primary sources and important secondary sources. Emphasis is on national sources. (Z7551.S84)

See also: A2−A3, and statistics under specific subject.

■B47 STUDY ABROAD

STUDY ABROAD (annual), International Documents. Handbook of fellowships, scholarships, and educational exchange. (LB2338.S86)

See also: B8, B15, B49.

SUMMER EMPLOYMENT

See: B23.

■B48 SYMBOLS AND SIGNS

CHRISTIAN SYMBOLS ANCIENT AND MODERN, 1973, Scribner's. (BU150.C53)

SHEPHERD'S GLOSSARY OF GRAPHIC SIGNS AND SYMBOLS, 1971, Dent. (AZ108.S53)

SYMBOL SOURCEBOOK: AN AUTHORITATIVE GUIDE TO INTERNATIONAL GRAPHIC SYMBOLS, 1972, McGraw-Hill. (AZ108.D74)

SYMBOLS, OUR UNIVERSAL LANGUAGE, by E.C. Hangen, 1963, McCormick-Armstrong. (CR29.H3)

SYMBOLS, SIGNS, AND THEIR MEANINGS, by A. Whittick, 1960, Leonard Hill. Covers visual symbols and symbolism. Emphasis on Western use and examples. (N7740.W52)

See also: A7.

TERM PAPERS

See: B22a

THESIS

See: B22a

■ B49 TRAVEL INFORMATION

WHOLE WORLD HANDBOOK: SIX CONTINENTS ON A STUDENT BUDGET, 1972– (annual), S and S. For student desiring to travel or study abroad. (LB2376.W48)

■ B50 UNITED STATES GOVERNMENT PUBLICATIONS

CATALOG OF THE PUBLIC DOCUMENTS OF CONGRESS AND OF ALL DEPARTMENTS OF THE GOVERNMENT OF THE UNITED STATES . . . 1893–1940, 40 vols., 1963 (reprint), Kraus Reprint. The permanent and complete catalog of all government publications since 1893. (Z1223.A13)

DOCUMENTS OFFICE CLASSIFICATION, 4th ed., 1974, U.S. Historical Documents Institute. May be useful for interlibrary loan. (Z697.G7P6)

GOVERNMENT PUBLICATIONS AND THEIR USE, 1969, Brookings Institution. (Z1223.Z7S3)

GOVERNMENT REFERENCE BOOKS, 3rd ed., 1974– (biennial), Libraries Unlimited. Annotated. (Z1223.Z7G68)

GUIDE TO U.S. GOVERNMENT PUBLICATIONS, 3 vols., 1973, Documents Index. (Z1223.Z7A5722)

LEGALLY AVAILABLE U.S. GOVERNMENT INFORMATION, 2 vols., 1970, Van Nos Reinhold. Tells how to secure information from the government under the Public Information Act. (KF5753.A33)

MONTHLY CATALOG OF U.S. GOVERNMENT PUBLICATIONS, 1941– (monthly). U.S. Government Printing Office. All publications issued by government bodies.

MONTHLY CATALOG OF U.S. GOVERNMENT PUBLICATIONS 1895–1962, 106 vols., 1974, Carrollton. (See Card Catalog)

THE NATIONAL UNION CATALOG OF U.S. GOVERNMENT PUBLICATIONS RECEIVED BY DEPOSITORY LIBRARIES, 4 vols., 1974. Carrollton. Excellent for interlibrary loan. (See Card Catalog)

SELECTED UNITED STATES GOVERNMENT PUBLICATIONS, 1968, Documents Index (Z1223.Z7D6)

SELECTED UNITED STATES GOVERNMENT PUBLICATIONS, 1928– (bi-weekly). U.S. Government Printing Office. A selected list of the more popular books and pamphlets.

SUBJECT GUIDE TO MAJOR UNITED STATES GOVERNMENT PUBLICATIONS, 1968, A.L.A. Annotated. (Z1223.Z7J32)

UNITED STATES GOVERNMENT PUBLICATIONS, 3rd ed., 1952, Wilson. Lists and describes important publications. (Z1223.Z7B7)

UNIVERSITIES

See: B15.

WORDS, ALL PROBLEMS

See: A7 and dictionaries under subject fields.

WRITING

See: B43.

■**B50a ADDITIONAL LISTS OF GENERAL REFERENCE WORKS**

AMERICAN REFERENCE BOOKS ANNUAL, 1970– (annual), Libraries Unlimited. (Z1035.1A55)

FUNDAMENTAL REFERENCE SOURCES, 1971, A.L.A. (Z1035.1C5)

GUIDE TO REFERENCE BOOKS, C. M. Winchell, 1967 and suppl., A.L.A. (Z1035.W79)

GUIDE TO REFERENCE MATERIALS, 3 vols. 3rd ed., 1973–, Bowker. (Z1035.W252)

THE READER'S ADVISER AND BOOKMAN'S MANUAL, 2 vols., 11th ed., 1968–69, Bowker. (Z1035.B7)

REFERENCE BOOKS IN PAPERBACK, 1972, Libraries Unlimited. (Z1035.1W95)

B51–B84 BUSINESS AND ECONOMICS

■**B51 ACCOUNTING**

ACCOUNTANT'S ENCYCLOPEDIA, 4 vols., 1962, Prentice-Hall. Not only for accountants but also for those seeking answers to accounting-related problems. Subjects grouped under ten sections. (HF5621.P7)

ACCOUNTANT'S HANDBOOK, 1970 (revised frequently) Ronald. Covers major phases of the field, basic data on current practices. (HF5621.A22)

ACCOUNTING DESK BOOK, 3rd ed., 1972, Institute for Business Planning. (HF5635.C33)

ACCOUNTING: INFORMATION SOURCES, 1970, Gale. Subject arrangement and annotations. (Z7164.C81D28)

A DICTIONARY FOR ACCOUNTANTS, 4th ed., 1969, Prentice-Hall. (HF5621.K6)

∎B51a   ASSOCIATIONS

WORLD GUIDE TO TRADE ASSOCIATIONS, 2 vols., 1973, Bowker. Professional organizations associated with trade and industry: unions, employees, chambers of commerce, etc. (See Card Catalog)

∎B52   ATLASES

ATLAS OF ECONOMIC DEVELOPMENT, 1961, University of Chicago. Shows world pattern of distribution of certain cultural, economic, and social factors by countries and regions. (G1046.G1G53)

ATLAS OF THE WORLD'S RESOURCES, 2 vols., 1952–1954, Prentice-Hall. Gives overall view of geographical distribution of mineral and agricultural products. (HC55.V3)

OXFORD ECONOMIC ATLAS OF THE WORLD, 4th ed., 1972, Oxford. The maps treat world production. (G1046.G1092)

RAND McNALLY COMMERCIAL ATLAS AND MARKETING GUIDE (annual), Rand McNally. Most extensive United States atlas, primarily for businessmen. Includes Canada. (G1200.R345)

BANKING

See: B62.

∎B53   BIBLIOGRAPHY

BUSINESS INFORMATION, HOW TO FIND AND USE IT, 1955, Harper. Listed by subject and annotated. Very good. (HF5353.M35)

ENCYCLOPEDIA OF BUSINESS INFORMATION SOURCES, 2 vols., 2nd ed., 1970, Gale. (HF5353.E52)

GUIDE TO BUSINESS HISTORY, 1958, Harvard. Comprehensive and annotated. (HC103.L3)

INTERNATIONAL BIBLIOGRAPHY OF ECONOMICS, 1952– (annual), Aldine. Paris UNESCO. Comprehensive. (Z7164. E2158)

A READER'S GUIDE TO THE SOCIAL SCIENCES, Rev. ed., 1970, Free Press. Covers most important classics in each field with comments. (H61.H69)

SOURCES OF BUSINESS INFORMATION, Revised, 1964, University of California Press. Covers many sources not directly related to business as well as standard sources. (Z7164.C81C75)

SOURCES OF INFORMATION IN THE SOCIAL SCIENCES, 2nd ed., 1973, ALA. (Z7161.W49)

■B54 BIOGRAPHY

POOR'S REGISTER OF DIRECTORS AND EXECUTIVES— UNITED STATES AND CANADA, 1928– (annual), Standard and Poor's Corporation. Most extensive guide to data on United States business executives. (HG4057.P6)

WHO'S WHO IN FINANCE AND INDUSTRY, , 1936– (biennial), Marquis. Sketches executives and key figures, emphasis on the United States. (HF3023.A2W5)

See also: A5–A6.

■B55 BUSINESS EDUCATION

EDUCATION INDEX, 1929–, Wilson. (Z5813.E23)

See also: B75.

■B56 BUSINESS HISTORY

GUIDE TO BUSINESS HISTORY, 1948, Harvard. Comprehensive and annotated. (HC103.L3)

See also: B66.

■B57 BUYING GUIDES

THE BUYING GUIDE ISSUE, CONSUMER REPORTS (annual), Consumers Union. Contains ratings of different products.

KELLY'S DIRECTORY OF MERCHANTS, MANUFACTURERS AND SHIPPERS, 1887– (annual), Kelly's Directories. Geographical arrangement. Lists merchants, manufacturers, exporters, agents, and so forth. Chiefly concerned with Great Britain. (HF54.G7K4)

MARCONI'S INTERNATIONAL REGISTER (annual), Telegraphic Cable and Radio Registration. Classified trades section. Covers principal firms of the world having international contacts. (HE7710.M3)

THOMAS' REGISTER OF AMERICAN MANUFACTURERS, 1905– (annual), Thomas. Most complete directory for the United States. (E302.J4632)

See also: B21, B58a.

◼B58   COMMERCE

COMMODITY YEAR BOOK, 1939– (annual), Commodity Research Bureau. (HF1041.C56)

RAND McNALLY COMMERCIAL ATLAS AND MARKETING GUIDE (annual), Rand McNally. Most extensive United States atlas, primarily for businessmen. Includes Canada. (G1200.R345)

See also: B63, B74.

◼B58a   CONSUMERS

CONSUMER SOURCEBOOK, 1974, Gale. Identifies prime information sources for the American consumer Indexes. (HC110.C63W37)

DIRECTORY OF GOVERNMENT AGENCIES SAFE-GUARDING CONSUMER AND ENVIRONMENT, 1968– (annual), Serina. (HC110.C6D5)

REFERENCE GUIDE FOR CONSUMERS, 1975, Bowker. Lists best publications on a subject and evaluation of each and organizations. Index included. (See Card Catalog)

◼B59   CORRESPONDENCE

BUSINESS EXECUTIVE'S HANDBOOK, 4th ed., 1953, Prentice-Hall. Provides answers to problems relating to selling, advertising, insurance, office management, credit, and collectors. (HF5356.B925)

See also: B81.

CURRENT INFORMATION
See: B18.

◼B60   DICTIONARIES

AMERICAN BUSINESS DICTIONARY, edited by H. Lazarus, 1957, Philosophical Library. (HB61.L3)

BUSINESS DICTIONARY, 1960, Prentice-Hall. (HF1002.N3)

DICTIONARY OF ECONOMICS, by H. Sloan, 5th ed., 1971, Barnes & Noble. (HB61.S54)

DICTIONARY OF ECONOMICS AND BUSINESS, by E. Nemmers, 1973, Littlefield. (HB61.N45)

DICTIONARY OF MODERN ECONOMICS, 2nd ed., 1973, McGraw-Hill. (HB61.M16)

ECONOMIC ALMANAC, 1940– (annual), National Industrial Conference Board. Glossary of selected terms. (HC101.E38)

DIRECTORIES

See: B21, B57.

■ **B61   ECONOMIC AREAS**

ECONOMIC AREAS OF THE UNITED STATES, 1961, Free Press. Covers areas larger than counties and smaller than states. Mostly statistics. (HC106.5.B568)

See also: B52.

■ **B62   FINANCE**

BANKING AND MONETARY STATISTICS, 1914–1941, 1943, Board of Governors of the Federal Reserve System. (HG2493.A52)

ENCYCLOPEDIA OF BANKING AND FINANCE, by G.G. Munn, 7th ed., 1973, Bankers Pub. Co. Comprehensive furnishing of explanations on some four thousand subjects. Useful bibliographies. (HG151.H8)

ENCYCLOPEDIC DICTIONARY OF BUSINESS FINANCES, 1960, Prentice-Hall. Comprehensive treatment of terms. Covers financial operations, methods, and practices. (HG151.P7)

FINANCIAL HANDBOOK, 4th ed., 1964, Ronald. Presents the many aspects of practical finance, including interest and annuity tables, discounts, and such. (HF5550.F5)

■ **B63   FOREIGN TRADE**

DIRECTORY OF UNITED STATES IMPORTERS, 1967– (annual), Journal of Commerce. Listing of importers and business information about them followed by an index showing what companies import which commodities. (See Card Catalog)

EXPORTER'S ENCYCLOPEDIA, 1904– (annual), Ashwell. Lists American and foreign trade organizations; gives steamship lines, shipping regulations, and so forth. (HF3011.E9)

FOREIGN COMMERCE YEARBOOK (annual), United States Department of Commerce. Detailed information on the foreign trade of the United States and other countries. (HF53.U72)

WORLD TRADE ANNUAL, 4 vols., 1963– (annual), Walker & Co. Comprehensive and detailed. (HF53.W6)

See also: B57.

■B64 GENERAL INFORMATION

BUSINESS FOUNDING DATE DICTIONARY, 1954, Morgan and Morgan. Covering 1687 to 1915, alphabetical and chronological lists. (HD2785.K4)

THE WORLD OF BUSINESS, by E.C. Bursk, 4 vols., 1963, Simon and Schuster. Writings and documents from earliest recorded times to the modern era. (HF5011.B75)

See also: A1–A4.

■B65 GOVERNMENT REPORTING

Commerce Clearing House and the Prentice-Hall "Services." Brings together all material bearing on a topic—discusses and interprets. Kept up to date by a loose-leaf service.

CONGRESSIONAL INDEX, 1937–, Commerce Clearing House. Records disposition of bills and resolutions introduced into Congress. Treaties also included. (J69.C6)

CONGRESSIONAL QUARTERLY ALMANAC, 1945– (annual and weekly), Congressional Quarterly, Inc. Presents facts on Congress and politics. Complete, concise, and unbiased. (JK1.C66)

■B66 HISTORICAL BACKGROUND

INTERNATIONAL ENCYCLOPEDIA OF THE SOCIAL SCIENCES, 17 vols., 1968, Macmillian. Covers most phases of social studies. (H40.A215)

ENCYCLOPEDIA OF THE SOCIAL SCIENCES, 15 vols., 1930–1935, Macmillan. Covers most phases of social studies. Useful but out-of-date. (H41.E8)

See also: A1, B56, B64.

INDEXES
See: B75.

■B67   INSURANCE

Best and Spectator "Services." Loose-leaf service.
DICTIONARY OF INSURANCE, 1970, Littlefield. (HG8025.D3)
HANDBOOK OF INSURANCE, by C.J. Crobaugh, 1949, Prentice-Hall. General information. (HG8025.C713)
INSURANCE: A GUIDE TO INFORMATION SOURCES, 1971, Gale. Briefly annotated. (Z7164.I7T48)
INSURANCE ALMANAC: WHO, WHAT, WHEN AND WHERE IN INSURANCE, 1912− (annual), Underwriter. (HG8019.I5)
LIFE INSURANCE FACT BOOK (annual), Institute of Life Insurance. Covers basic facts and figures. Starts with 1890. (HG8943.L5)

■B68   INVESTMENTS

BEST BOOKS ON THE STOCK MARKET, 1972, Bowker. Annotated. (Z7164.F5Z46)
INVESTMENT COMPANIES (annual), Arthur and Company. Valuable compendium of information on investment companies and mutual funds. (HG4530.I52)
Moody's and Standard and Poor's "Services." Loose-leaf services.

■B69   LABOR

DIRECTORY OF NATIONAL UNIONS AND EMPLOYEE ASSOCIATIONS, 1971− U.S. Govt. Printing Office. Covers a variety of information. (HD6504.A15)
HISTORY OF LABOUR IN THE UNITED STATES, by J.R. Commons, 4 vols., 1935−1951, Macmillan. (HD8066.C7)
BNA POLICY AND PRACTICE SERIES (annual service), Bureau of National Affairs. Guide to successful employer−employee relations. Contains many case histories. (HD4802.L44)

■B70   LAW

BLACKS LAW DICTIONARY, 1970, West. Highly respected work. (KB62.B5)
LAW IN THE UNITED STATES OF AMERICA: A SELECTIVE BIBLIOGRAPHICAL GUIDE, 1966, N.Y.U. Pr. (KF1.Z9A65)
THE LAWYER'S ENCYCLOPEDIA, 1963, Prentice-Hall. (K.L36)
See also: A7, B150.

■B71   LEGAL REPORTING

Commerce Clearing House and the Prentice-Hall "Services." Brings together all material bearing on a topic, discusses, and interprets. Kept up to date by a loose-leaf service.

■B72   LOCAL INFORMATION

City Directories (usually annual).

MUNICIPAL YEARBOOK (annual), Inter-City Managers Association. Data of all kinds on medium-sized and large cities and towns in the United States. Includes directory of major officials of city governments. (JS344.C5)

See also: B32, B161.

■B73   MANAGEMENT

BUSINESS EXECUTIVES HANDBOOK, 4th ed., 1953, Prentice-Hall. Designed to provide answers to management problems. (HF5356.B925)

ENCYCLOPEDIA OF MANAGEMENT, 2nd ed., 1973, Van Nos Reinhold. (HD19.H4)

See also: B64, B69.

MANUFACTURER'S ADDRESSES
See: B8.

■B74   MARKETING

CENSUS OF BUSINESS, U.S. Government Printing Office. (See Card Catalog)

RAND McNALLY COMMERCIAL ATLAS AND MARKETING GUIDE (annual), Rand McNally. Maps cover transportation, retail trade, mining, manufacturing, and so forth. (G1200. R345)

■B75   PERIODICAL INDEXES

BUSINESS PERIODICALS INDEX, 1958–, Wilson. Covers fields of accounting, advertising, banking and finance, labor, and so forth. (Z7164.C81B983)

INDEX OF ECONOMIC JOURNALS, 1886–1966, 8 vols., 1966, American Economic Association. Very comprehensive. (Z7164.E2I48)

INDUSTRIAL ARTS INDEX, 1913–1957, Wilson. Covers economics, business and finance, management, insurance, and so forth. Divided into two publications: APPLIED

SCIENCE AND TECHNOLOGY INDEX, 1958–, and
BUSINESS PERIODICAL INDEX, 1958–. (Z913.I7)
THE NEW YORK TIMES INDEX, 1851–, The New York Times.
General. (AI21.N44)
PUBLIC AFFAIRS INFORMATION SERVICE BULLETIN,
1915–, Public Affairs Information Service. Good for
economics. (Z7163.P9)
READERS' GUIDE TO PERIODICAL LITERATURE, 1900–,
Wilson. General. (AI3.R496)
SOCIAL SCIENCES INDEX, 1974–, Wilson. (Formally called
SOCIAL SCIENCES AND HUMANITIES INDEX. Good for
economics. (See Card Catalog)
WALL STREET JOURNAL INDEX (monthly), Wall Street Jour-
nal. (HG1.W26)

■B76 PERSONNEL

HANDBOOK OF PERSONNEL MANAGEMENT, 1953, Harper.
Methods for organization of fewer than three thousand
employees. (HF5549.H278)
PERSONNEL HANDBOOK, 1951, Ronald. Practical guide for
companies of varying sizes. (HF5549.M34)

■B77 PLACEMENT

POOR'S REGISTER OF DIRECTORS AND EXECUTIVES (annual). Standard and Poor's Corporation. Most extensive guide
to data on United States business executives. (HG4057.P6)
See also: B23.

B78 POPULATION

CENSUS OF POPULATION, 1961–, U.S. Government Printing
Office. (See Card Catalog)
See also: B46, B82.

■B79 PRODUCTION

CENSUS OF AGRICULTURE, U.S. Government Printing Office.
(See Card Catalog)
CENSUS OF MANUFACTURES, U.S. Government Printing
Office. (See Card Catalog)
COMMODITY YEAR BOOK, 1939– (annual), Commodity
Research Bureau. Covers about one hundred basic com-

modities with tables, charts, and some feature articles.
(HF1041.C56)
See also: B75.

■B80   REAL ESTATE

ENCYCLOPEDIC DICTIONARY OF REAL ESTATE
PRACTICE, 2nd ed., 1963, Prentice-Hall. Discussions of
almost all terms used in real estate business. (HD1375.P67)

■B81   SECRETARIAL INFORMATION

COMPLETE SECRETARY'S HANDBOOK, 3rd ed., 1970,
Prentice-Hall. (HF5547.D62)
THE PRIVATE SECRETARY'S MANUAL, 3rd ed., 1963,
Prentice-Hall. (HF5547.T8)
SECRETARY'S HANDBOOK, 9th ed., rev., 1969, Macmillan.
Emphasizes correct English usage. (HF5547.T25)
STANDARD HANDBOOK FOR SECRETARIES, 8th ed., 1969,
McGraw-Hill. (HF5547.H77)

■B82   STATISTICS

ECONOMIC ALMANAC, 1940– (annual), National Industrial
Conference Board. Covers almost every phase of business and
allied subjects in the United States. Compact and
trustworthy. Very useful. (HC101.E38)
ECONOMIC AREAS OF THE UNITED STATES, 1961, Free
Press. Covers areas larger than counties and smaller than
states. (HC106.5.B568)
HANDBOOK OF BASIC ECONOMIC STATISTICS, 1947–,
Government Statistic Bureau. Monthly publication giving
latest statistics of United States economic life. (HC101.H25)
See also: A2–A3, B46, B158, B161.

■B83   TAXES

FEDERAL TAX HANDBOOK (annual), Prentice-Hall. Shortcut
guide to an understanding of the Internal Revenue Code as
last amended and to the solution of personal and business
income-tax problems. (HJ3252.P686)
FEDERAL TAXES (annual), Commerce Clearing House. Gives
basic principles of federal income-tax laws. (HJ2381.K7)
PRENTICE-HALL FEDERAL TAX COURSE (annual), Prentice-
Hall. A student's edition; an abbreviation of the following
work: (HJ4652.A7P6)

PRENTICE-HALL FEDERAL TAXES (annual and supplements), Prentice-Hall. A loose-leaf service covering new laws, new regulations, administrative interpretations, and judicial decisions. (HJ4652.P8)

STANDARD FEDERAL TAX REPORTER (annual and supplements), Commerce Clearing House. Loose-leaf service covering full treatment of income-tax problems. (HJ3251.A3C6)

TRADE
See: B63.

UNIONS
See: B69.

■B84 UNITED NATIONS

YEARBOOK OF THE UNITED NATIONS, 1947– (annual), United Nations. Lists its activities, texts of documents, publications, and some biographical material. (JX1977.A37A4)

B85–B114 EDUCATION, PSYCHOLOGY, AND PHYSICAL EDUCATION

■B85 ADDRESSES OF ASSOCIATIONS AND ORGANIZATIONS

EDUCATION DIRECTORY, 1912–, part IV (annual), U.S. Government Printing Office, (L111.A6)

MEMBERSHIP DIRECTORY, (annual), American Psychiatric Association. (RC335.A55)

MEMBERSHIP REGISTER, (annual), American Psychological Association. (BF30.A49)

NEA HANDBOOK FOR LOCAL, STATE, AND NATIONAL ASSOCIATIONS (biennial), National Education Association. (L13.N4625)

■B85a ADULT EDUCATION

THE NEW YORK TIMES GUIDE TO CONTINUING EDUCATION IN AMERICA, 1972, Quadrangle. Adult courses, academic and vocational, offered at accredited educational institutions. (L901.C74)

AUDIO-VISUAL AIDS
See: B9, B109.

■ B86   BIBLIOGRAPHY

BIBLIOGRAPHIES AND SUMMARIES IN EDUCATION TO JULY 1935, 1936, Wilson. Indispensable for locating educational bibliographies between 1910 and 1935. (Z5811.A1.M69)

NON-FORMAL EDUCATION, AN ANNOTATED INTERNATIONAL BIBLIOGRAPHY, 1972, Praeger. (Z5811.P27)

SOURCES OF INFORMATION IN THE SOCIAL SCIENCES, 2nd ed., 1973, ALA. (Z7161.W49)

See also: B11.

■ B87   BIOGRAPHY

THE ACADEMIC WHO'S WHO, 1973, (biennially), Bowker. Covers British Isles in the arts, education, and social sciences. (L915.A658)

CYCLOPEDIA OF EDUCATION, 5 vols., 1911–1913, Macmillan. Now out of date but good for biography, history, and philosophy of education. (LB15.M6)

DIRECTORY OF AMERICAN SCHOLARS, 4 vols., 6th ed., 1974, Bowker. Sketches of contemporary scholars in the humanities and social sciences. (LA2311.W45)

LEADERS IN EDUCATION, 4th ed., 1971, Bowker. Concise information about foremost educators. (LA2311.L4)

OUTSTANDING COLLEGE ATHLETES OF AMERICA, (annual). Outstanding college athletes of America. (GV697.A1086)

WHO'S WHO IN AMERICAN COLLEGE AND UNIVERSITY ADMINISTRATION, 1970, Crowell-Collier Educational Corp. (LA2311.P72)

WHO'S WHO IN AMERICAN EDUCATION, 1928– (alternate years) Who's Who in American Education, Inc. Prominent educators. (LA2311.W45)

See also: A5–A6, B98.

■ B88   CERTIFICATION

A MANUAL ON CERTIFICATION REQUIREMENTS FOR SCHOOL PERSONNEL IN THE UNITED STATES, 1951–

(biennial), National Education Association. (LB1771.M3)
REQUIREMENTS FOR CERTIFICATION, 1955– (annual),
University of Chicago. (LB1771.W6)
Also: Write directly to individual state education offices for complete information.
See: B85.

■ **B89 CHILDREN'S LITERATURE**

EDUCATION INDEX, 1929–, Wilson. (Z5813.E123)
See also: B98, B175, B186.

BIBLIOGRAPHY
CHILDREN'S CATALOG. 12th ed., 1971, and supplements,
Wilson. A classified list with annotations. (Z1037.W76)
GOOD BOOKS FOR CHILDREN, 3rd ed., 1950–1965, By M.K.
Eakin, 1966, University of Chicago. Selective list of books in
print. Evaluated and annotated. (Z1037.E15)
SUBJECT AND TITLE INDEX TO SHORT STORIES FOR
CHILDREN, 1955, American Library Association. For use
with children in grades 3 to 9. (Z1037.A4924)

COLLEGE AND UNIVERSITY INFORMATION
See: B15, B30.

■ **B90 COMPARATIVE EDUCATION**

EDUCATIONAL YEARBOOK, 1924–1926 and 1927–1944, Macmillan. Early volumes contain articles arranged by countries;
after 1930, devoted mainly to some particular aspect of education. (L11.E52)
WORLD SURVEY OF EDUCATION, 5 vols., 1956–1971,
UNESCO. Gives descriptive and statistical information on
education in all countries and territories of the world.
(L900.W56)
THE WORLD YEARBOOK OF EDUCATION, Harcourt (formerly
YEARBOOK OF EDUCATION). Contains surveys of education monthly in English-speaking countries. (L101.G8Y4)
See also: A1–A3.

■ **B91 DICTIONARIES**

DICTIONARY OF EDUCATION, by C. Good, 1973, McGraw-Hill.
Covers whole range of education, including selected terms
from philosophy, psychology, and sociology. (LB15.G6)

PSYCHIATRIC DICTIONARY, 4th ed., 1970, Oxford. Not only defines but also includes explanations. (RC437.H5)

▪B92 DIRECTORIES

GUIDE TO AMERICAN EDUCATIONAL DIRECTORIES, 3rd ed., 1969, McGraw-Hill. Good for all phases of education. (Z5813.G8)

THE NATIONAL FACULTY DIRECTORY, 1970– (annual), Gale. Inclusive list of full-time faculty, lecturers, and other full-time personnel. (L901.N34)

▪B93 DISSERTATIONS

MASTER'S THESES IN EDUCATION, 1953–, Research Publications. (Z5816.I6M3)
See also: B22.

▪B93a DOCUMENTATION

DOCUMENTATION IN EDUCATION, Burke, 1967, Teachers College. (Z711.B93)
See also: B22a.

▪B94 EDUCATION—HISTORY

GUIDE TO RESEARCH IN EDUCATIONAL HISTORY, by W.W. Brickman, 1949, New York University. The standard work on historiography as applied to educational research. (LA9.B7)
See also: B98.

EDUCATORS
See: B87.

▪B95 ELEMENTARY EDUCATION

BASIC BOOK COLLECTION FOR ELEMENTARY GRADES, 7th ed., 1960, American Library Association. Brief annotations given. (Z1037.B3)

THE ELEMENTARY SCHOOL LIBRARY COLLECTION: A GUIDE TO BOOKS AND OTHER MEDIA, 1970, Bro-Dart Foundation. Codes given for grade level. Indexes. (Z1037.E4)
See also: B90, B98.

■B96   EXCEPTIONAL CHILDREN

DIRECTORY FOR EXCEPTIONAL CHILDREN, 7th ed., 1972, Sargent. Lists private and state schools, guidance clinics, and so forth. (LC4007.D5)

■B97   FEDERAL GOVERNMENT AND EDUCATION

CONGRESSIONAL QUARTERLY ALMANAC, 1945– (weekly and annually), Congressional Quarterly, Inc. Good for current issues before Congress dealing with education. Complete, concise, and unbiased. (JK1.C66)
See also: B101, B107.

FELLOWSHIPS
See: B45.

FILMS
See: B9.

■B98   GENERAL WORKS

CYCLOPEDIA OF EDUCATION, 5 vols., 1911-1913, Macmillan. Out of date but good for history and philosophy of education. (LB15.M6)
THE ENCYCLOPEDIA OF EDUCATION, 10 vols., 1971, Macmillan. Comprehensive coverage, primarily of American education giving an overall view of a topic. (LB15.E47)
ENCYCLOPEDIA OF EDUCATIONAL RESEARCH, 4th ed., 1969, Macmillan. Articles on educational research by experts. (LB15.E48)
WORLD SURVEY OF EDUCATION, 5 vols., 1956–1971, UNESCO. Gives descriptive and statistical information on all countries. (L900.W56)
See also: A1–A3.

■B99   HANDICRAFTS

HANDBOOK OF HOBBIES AND CRAFTS, 1975, Bowker. Guide to Leisure time activities providing description of each, history, relevant associations, clubs, plus a bibliography. (See Card Caralog)
INDEX TO HANDICRAFTS, MODELMAKING, AND WORKSHOP PROJECTS, 1936–1974, 6 vols., 1975, Faxon. Helps answer "How to make it" questions. (Z7911.L89)

HIGH SCHOOL
See: B101, B103.

■B100   HIGHER EDUCATION

WORLD SURVEY OF EDUCATION, 5 vols., 1956–1971, Vol. IV, UNESCO. Gives descriptive and statistical information on all countries. (L900.W56)

YEARBOOK OF HIGHER EDUCATION, 1970– (annual), Academic Press. Directory of higher education and statistics of higher education. (LB2300.Y4)

See also: A1, B15, B98, B101.

■B101   INDEXES

COMPLETE GUIDE AND INDEX TO ERIC REPORTS THRU DECEMBER 1969, 1970, Prentice-Hall. Includes 24,558 documents. (Z5814.R4C6)

EDUCATION INDEX, 1929–, Wilson. A subject and author index to educational periodicals, books, pamphlets, monographs, and reports. (Z5813.E23)

ERIC (Educational Research Information Center), 1964–, U.S. Govt. Pr. Off. An abstracting service on microfiche cards. It is the most comprehensive collection of documents on educational research. (Z5811.R4)

HISTORICAL ABSTRACTS, 1955–, International Social Science Institute. Useful in extensive research. (D299.H5)

THE NEW YORK TIMES INDEX, 1851–, The New York Times. Current education news and exhaustive coverage of sports events. (AI21.N44)

PSYCHOLOGICAL ABSTRACTS, 1927–, American Psychological Association. Covers all phases of psychology. (BF1.P65)

PSYCHOLOGICAL INDEX, 1895–1936, Psychological Review Co. An annual bibliography of the literature of psychology and related subjects. (Z7203.P97)

READERS' GUIDE TO PERIODICAL LITERATURE, 1900–, Wilson. Covers general information. (AI3.R496)

STATE EDUCATION JOURNAL INDEX, 1963– (semiannual), Ratliff. Covers state and association publications. (Z5811.S7)

■B102   INTERMEDIATE GRADES

SUBJECT INDEX TO BOOKS FOR INTERMEDIATE

GRADES, 3rd ed., 1963, American Library Association. Listed by subject with brief annotations. (Z1037.E16)

■B103   JUNIOR HIGH SCHOOL

BASIC BOOK COLLECTION FOR JUNIOR HIGH SCHOOLS, 3rd ed., 1960, American Library Association. Includes a list of recommended periodicals. (Z1037.B34)
See also: B114.

LAW
See: B107.

■B104   MENTAL HEALTH

ENCYCLOPEDIA OF MENTAL HEALTH, 6 vols., 1963, Watts. Integrated, up-to-date information including glossary and bibliographic section. (RA790.E56)
See also: B101.

PHYSICAL EDUCATION
See: A1—A3, B98, B101, B110.

■B105   PRIMARY EDUCATION

SUBJECT INDEX TO BOOKS FOR PRIMARY GRADES, 1961, American Library Association. Listed by subject with brief annotations. (Z1037.E17)
WORLD SURVEY OF EDUCATION, 5 vols., 1956–1971, Vol. II, UNESCO. Gives descriptive and statistical information on all countries. (L900.W56)

■B106   PSYCHOLOGY

ANNUAL REVIEW OF PSYCHOLOGY, 1950–, Annual Reviews. Covers new developments in the field. (BF30.A56)
DICTIONARY OF BEHAVIORAL SCIENCE, 1973, Van Nostrand Reinhold. (BF31.W64)
THE ENCYCLOPEDIA OF PHILOSOPHY, 8 vols., 1967, Macmillan. Includes good articles in the field of psychology. (B41.E5)
ENCYCLOPEDIA OF PSYCHOLOGY, 3 vols., 1972, Herder and Herder. Short and long articles. Bibliographies. (BF31.E522)
THE LANGUAGE OF PSYCHOANALYSIS, 1974, Norton. An annotated dictionary of terms. (RC437.L313)

PERSONALITY: TESTS AND REVIEWS, 1970, Gryphon. Covers up to mid-1969. (BF698.5B87)
See also: A1, B98, B101, B113.

BIBLIOGRAPHY
THE HARVARD LIST OF BOOKS OF PSYCHOLOGY, 4th ed., 1971, Harvard. A selective list with brief comments. (Z7201.H28)
See also: B11.

■B106a   RECORDS AND TAPES

INDEX TO EDUCATIONAL AUDIO TAPES, 2nd ed., 1972, NICEM. 18,000 entries. (LB1044.4.Z9N3)
INDEX TO EDUCATIONAL RECORDS, 2nd ed., 1972, NICEM. 16,000 records. (LB1044.3.Z9N33)
See also: B109, B133.

RECREATION
See: A1–A3, B98, B101, B110.

■B107   SCHOOL LAW

YEARBOOK OF SCHOOL LAW, 1933– (annual), Interstate Printers and Publishers, Inc. Includes digests of court decisions affecting schools. (L101.U5Y4)

■B108   SECONDARY EDUCATION

BASIC BOOK COLLECTION FOR HIGH SCHOOLS, 7th ed., 1963, American Library Association. Classified and annotated list. (Z1037.B33)
SENIOR HIGH SCHOOL LIBRARY CATALOG, 10th ed., 1972 and suppls., Wilson. A classified and annotated list. (Z1035.S42)
WORLD SURVEY OF EDUCATION, 5 vols., 1956–1971, Vol. III, UNESCO. Gives descriptive and statistical information on all countries. (L900.W56)
See also: B101.

■B109   SOURCEBOOKS

AUDIOVISUAL MARKET PLACE, 1969– (annual), Bowker. A directory of producers, suppliers of A-V media and equipment. Index. (LB1043.A817)

EDUCATIONAL MEDIA YEARBOOK, 1973–, Bowker. Comprehensive in coverage. (LB1028.3.E37)

EDUCATORS GUIDES TO FREE FILMS; Filmstrips; Guidance Materials; Health, Physical Education and Recreation Materials; Science Materials; Social Studies Materials; Tapes, Scripts and Transcriptions; Curriculum Materials; (annuals), Educators Progress Service. These are all separate titles (8) from the same publisher. All are annotated.

FREE AND INEXPENSIVE LEARNING MATERIALS, 1941– (biennial), George Peabody College for Teachers. (Z5817.2.G4)

GUIDE TO NEWER EDUCATIONAL MEDIA, 1961, American Library Association. (Z5814.V8R8)

HOW TO LOCATE EDUCATIONAL INFORMATION, AN AID TO QUICK UTILIZATATION OF THE LITERATURE OF EDUCATION, 4th ed., 1962, Teachers College, Columbia. (Z711.A37)

RESOURCES FOR EDUCATORS, 1974, Bowker. Comprehensive guide to non-print media for pre-service and in-service instruction. Includes descriptive details. (See Card Catalog)
See also: B9.

■ B110   SPORTS

THE DICTIONARY OF SPORTS, by P. Cummings, 1949, Ronald. (GV567.C85)

ENCYCLOPEDIA OF SPORT SCIENCES AND MEDICINE, 1971, Macmillan. Authoritative and comprehensive. (RC1210.E5)

THE ENCYCLOPEDIA OF SPORTS, 1969, A.S. Barnes. The most complete and authoritative source on sports in America and Europe. (GV11.M4)

RULES OF THE GAME: THE COMPLETE ILLUSTRATED ENCYCLOPEDIA OF ALL THE SPORTS OF THE WORLD, 1974, Paddington. Covers same 150 sports and sporting events. Well illustrated. (GV731.D52)

SPORTS RULES ENCYCLOPEDIA, 1961, National Press. Covers official rules for thirty-eight sports and games. (GV731.S75)
See also: A1–A3, B98.

■ B111 STATISTICS

DIGEST OF EDUCATIONAL STATISTICS, 1962– (annual), U.S. Government Printing Office. Covers all levels of American education of current interests and values that are nationwide in scope. (L112.A35)

WORLD SURVEY OF EDUCATION, 5 vols., 1956–1971, UNESCO. Gives descriptive and statistical information on all countries. (L900.W56)

See also: B46.

■ B112 SUPERINTENDENTS

EDUCATION DIRECTORY, 1912– (annual), Part 2, U.S. Government Printing Office. Names and addresses. (L111.A6)

■ B113 TESTING

MENTAL MEASUREMENT YEARBOOK, 6th ed., 1965, Gryphon Press. Stresses test developments in the period since the publication of the last volume. All volumes are useful. (Z5814.P8B932)

PERSONALITY: TESTS AND REVIEWS, 1970. Gryphon. Covers up to mid-1969. (BF698.5B87)

TEST AND MEASUREMENTS IN CHILD DEVELOPMENT, 1971, Jossey-Bass. It does not overlap the MENTAL MEASUREMENTS YEARBOOK. (BF722.J64)

TESTS IN PRINT: A COMPREHENSIVE BIBLIOGRAPHY OF TESTS FOR USE IN EDUCATION, PSYCHOLOGY, AND INDUSTRY, 1961, Gryphon Press. The only comprehensive bibliography of its kind. This is also an index to the tests found in the MENTAL MEASUREMENT YEARBOOK. (Z5814.P8B932)

■ B114 TEXTBOOKS

TEXTBOOKS IN PRINT (annual), 1871–, Bowker. Covers elementary, junior, senior high-school textbooks, and some professional books for teachers. (Z5813.A51)

B115–138 FINE ARTS (Art, Music, and Speech)

■ **B115   ARCHITECTS**

AMERICAN ARCHITECTS DIRECTORY, 3rd ed., 1970, Bowker.
Brief biographical data. (NA53.A37)
BIOGRAPHICAL DICTIONARY OF AMERICAN
ARCHITECTS, 1740–1952, by H.F. Withey, 1971,
Hennessey. Complements the AMERICAN ARCHITECTS
DIRECTORY. (NA736.W57)
A BIOGRAPHICAL DICTIONARY OF ENGLISH ARCHITECTS,
1660–1840, by H.M. Colvin, 1954, Harvard University.
Valuable and scholarly. Includes indexes of persons and
places. (NA996.C6)

■ **B116   ARCHITECTURE**

DICTIONARY OF ARCHITECTURAL SCIENCE, 1973, Halsted.
(NA31.C64)
HOW TO FIND OUT IN ARCHITECTURE AND BUILDING, A
GUIDE TO SOURCES OF INFORMATION, 1966, Pergamon
Press. International in scope. (Z5941.S58)
THE PELICAN HISTORY OF ART, 50 vols., 1953–, Penguin.
Comprehensive and scholarly guide to world art and architecture. Each volume is devoted to a particular area.
See also: A1, B117.

■ **B117   ART**

BIBLIOGRAPHY

GUIDE TO ART REFERENCE BOOKS, 1959, American Library
Association. Covers architecture, painting, sculpture, prints,
engravings, and drawings. Annotated. (Z5931.C45)

BIOGRAPHY

AMERICAN ART DIRECTORY, 1898–, Bowker. Mainly institutional information. Also includes scholarships and
fellowship information. (N50.A54)
DICTIONARY OF ARTISTS IN AMERICA, 1564–1860, 1957,
Yale. Covers painters, draftsmen, sculptors, engravers, and
others in the field. Scholarly. (N6536.N4)
DICTIONARY OF BRITISH SCULPTORS, 1660–1851, by R.
Gunnis, 1953, Harvard. Scholarly and useful, including good
indexes by subject and place. (NB496.G85)
DICTIONARY OF CONTEMPORARY AMERICAN ARTISTS,
2nd ed., 1971, St. Martin's. Covers most important artists.
(N6536.C8)

INDEX OF ARTISTS, INTERNATIONAL-BIOGRAPHICAL, 1935 (1948), supplement, 1940 (1948), P. Smith. An index to biographical material about artists of all countries. (N40.M3)

WHO'S WHO IN AMERICAN ART, 1935—, Bowker. Biographical directory of contemporary artists, editors, critics. (N6536.W6)

WHO'S WHO IN ART, 1927— (irregularly), Art Trade Press. Biographies of leading men and women in the world of art today. (N40.W6)

See also: A5—A6, B130.

GENERAL WORKS

ADELINE'S ART DICTIONARY, 1953, J.W. Edwards. Concise definitions of all terms. (N33.A223)

APOLLO: AN ILLUSTRATED MANUAL OF THE HISTORY OF ART THROUGHOUT THE AGES . . . , 1935, Scribner. (N5300.R56)

A DICTIONARY OF COLOR, by A. Maerz, 1950, McGraw-Hill. Names of colors with color reproductions. (QC495.M25)

ENCYCLOPEDIA OF WORLD ART, 15 vols., 1959—68, McGraw-Hill. Comprehensive guide to world art including biographies. (N31.E4833)

EVERYMAN'S DICTIONARY OF PICTORIAL ART, 2 vols., 1962, Dutton. (N31.G3)

GLOSSARY OF ART, ARCHITECTURE AND DESIGN SINCE 1945, 1973, Linnet Books. (N34.W34)

THE OXFORD COMPANION TO ART, 1970, Oxford. (N33.09)

THE PELICAN HISTORY OF ART, 50 vols., 1953—, Penguin. Comprehensive and scholarly guide to world art and architecture. (See Card Catalog)

REINHOLD COLOR ATLAS, 1962, Reinhold. Very useful guide to color matching. (ND1285.K6)

See also: A1, B131.

HISTORY

ART THROUGH THE AGES, 1970, Harcourt. A good survey. (N5300.G25)

See also: B117, and General Works under Art.

INDEXES

THE AMERICAN LIBRARY COMPENDIUM AND INDEX OF WORLD ART, 1961, American Library Color Slide Co. Comprehensive listing of the historically important art of all periods, areas, media, and styles. (N4040.A45)

ART INDEX, 1929–, Wilson. Covers periodicals and museum publications. (Z5937.A78)

EDUCATION INDEX, 1929, Wilson. Good for subjects on teaching of fine arts. (Z5813.E23)

THE NEW YORK TIMES INDEX, 1851–, The New York Times. Useful for current information. (AI21.N44)

READERS' GUIDE TO PERIODICAL LITERATURE, 1900, Wilson. General information. (AI3.R496)

See also: B132.

■ B118   BALLET

A DICTIONARY OF BALLET TERMS, 3rd ed., 1974, Pitman. (GV1585.K45)

DICTIONARY OF MODERN BALLET, 1959, Tudor. Covers history, repertoire, and personalities of contemporary ballet. (GV1787.D513)

See also: B127.

■ B119   BIBLIOGRAPHY, GENERAL

RELIGIONS, MYTHOLOGIES, FOLKLORE, 1962, Scarecrow. Covers fine arts. (Z7751.D54)

See also: B11 and under specific subject.

■ B119a   BIOGRAPHY—GENERAL

INDEX TO ARTISTIC BIOGRAPHY, 2 vols., 1973, Scarecrow. Covers some 70,000 artists. (N40.H38)

See also: Individual subject and A5, A6, B11a.

■ B120   CHILDREN'S SONGS

CHILDREN'S SONG INDEX, 1936, H.W. Wilson. By titles, authors, composers, subjects, and first lines. (ML128.S3C9)

COMPOSERS

See: B127.

■ B121   CONCERT MUSIC

ENCYCLOPEDIA OF CONCERT MUSIC, by D. Ewen, 1959, Hill and Wang. General Information. (ML100.E85)

See also: B127.

COSTUME

See: B177.

DIALOGS
See: B125.

DRAMA
See: B138, B180.

HANDICRAFTS
See: B99.

■ **B122 ILLUSTRATIONS**

ILLUSTRATION INDEX, 3rd ed., 1973, Scarecrow. Indexes illustrations in various magazines. (N7525.G72)
INDEX TO ILLUSTRATIONS, 1967, Faxon. Guide to pictures in books and magazines. (NC996.E62)
See also: B40a, B132.

■ **B123 ILLUSTRATORS OF CHILDREN'S BOOKS**

ILLUSTRATORS OF CHILDREN'S BOOKS, 1744-1945, 1947 (supplements cover 1946−1966), Horn. Very complete, including biographies, bibliographies, and so forth. (NC965.M32)

■ **B124 JAZZ**

ENCYCLOPEDIA OF JAZZ, 1960 (revised frequently under various titles), Horizon. General information including biographies of jazz celebrities. (Issued under various titles.) (ML3561.J3E55)
THE LITERATURE OF JAZZ; A CRITICAL GUIDE, 1970, A.L.A. Covers the entire spectrum of publications on jazz. (ML128.J3K45)

■ **B125 MONOLOGS AND DIALOGS**

INDEX TO MONOLOGS AND DIALOGS, 1949, supplement 1959, Faxon. (PN4305.M6I64)

MUSEUMS
See: B35.

■ **B127 MUSIC**

BIBLIOGRAPHY
A BIBLIOGRAPHY OF EARLY SECULAR AMERICAN MUSIC, 1945, Library of Congress. (ML120.U586)

A BIBLIOGRAPHY OF NORTH AMERICAN FOLKLORE AND
FOLKSONG, by C. Haywood, 1951, Dover. Descriptive and
evaluative annotations. (Z5984.U5H3)
A GUIDE TO REFERENCE MATERIALS ON MUSIC, 3rd ed.,
1955, University of California Press. Prepared for the
researcher using the library. (LD744.A3)
HISTORICAL SETS, COLLECTED EDITIONS, AND
MONUMENTS OF MUSIC, 2nd ed., 1969, A.L.A.
(ML113.H52)
A LIST OF BOOKS ABOUT MUSIC IN THE ENGLISH
LANGUAGE, by P.A. Scholes, 1940, Oxford University Press.
(ML100.S3709)
MUSIC REFERENCE AND RESEARCH MATERIALS: AN
ANNOTATED BIBLIOGRAPHY, 3rd ed., 1974, Free Press.
(ML113.D83)
SCHIRMER'S GUIDE TO BOOKS ON MUSIC AND
MUSICIANS, by R.D. Darrell, 1951, Schirmer. Annotated.
(ML113.D3)
See also: B11.

BIOGRAPHY
AMERICAN COMPOSERS TODAY, by D. Ewen, 1949, Wilson.
Includes the United States and Latin America, and European
composers who live in the Americas. (ML390.E82)
THE ASCAP BIOGRAPHICAL DICTIONARY OF COMPOSERS,
AUTHORS, AND PUBLISHERS, 2nd ed., 1952, Crowell and
Ambassador. Sketches of each. (ML106.U3A5)
BAKER'S BIOGRAPHICAL DICTIONARY OF MUSICIANS, 5th
ed., 1958, and suppl. 1971, Schirmer. Covers musicians of all
nations. (ML105.B16)
BIO-BIBLIOGRAPHICAL INDEX OF MUSICIANS IN THE
UNITED STATES OF AMERICA FROM COLONIAL
TIMES . . . , 1941, Pan American Union. (ML106.U3H6)
BIOGRAPHICAL DICTIONARY OF COMPOSERS, by P.M.
Young, 1954, Crowell. Brief sketches of composers past and
present. (ML390.Y6)
THE BOOK OF MODERN COMPOSERS, 1950, Knopf and
McClelland. (ML390.E83)
COMPOSERS IN AMERICA, by C.R. Reis, 1947, Macmillan.
Contemporary composers in the United States, with lists of
their works. (ML390.R38)

COMPOSERS OF OPERETTA, 1962, St. Martin's. (ML390.H887C6)

COMPOSERS OF YESTERDAY, by D. Ewen, 1937, Wilson. Chiefly those who lived before the twentieth century. (ML105.E94C62)

COMPOSERS SINCE 1900, 1970, Wilson. 220 twentieth-century composers. (ML390.E833)

EUROPEAN COMPOSERS TODAY, by D. Ewen, 1954, Wilson. Covers best known contemporary European composers, with many portraits. (ML390.E834)

FAMOUS COMPOSERS AND THEIR WORKS, by J.K. Paine, 4 vols., 1891, Millet. (M1.F17)

INDEX TO BIOGRAPHIES OF CONTEMPORARY COMPOSERS, 2 vols., 1964, 1974, Scarecrow. A good starting point for information. (ML105.B9)

LIVING MUSICIANS, by D. Ewen, 1940, supplement 1957, Wilson. Contemporary musicians with many portraits. (ML105.E95)

NEW BOOK OF MODERN COMPOSERS, 1961, Knopf. (ML390.E83)

THE NEW ENCYCLOPEDIA OF MUSIC AND MUSICIANS, by W. Pratt, 1956, Macmillan. Three sections: musicial terms and forms; biographical; and musical organizations and institutions. (ML100.P87)

NEW ENCYCLOPEDIA OF THE GREAT COMPOSERS AND THEIR MUSIC, 2 vols., 1969, Doubleday. Consists of composers, past and present, who have contributed most to the history of music. Also includes a brief history of music, one hundred basic records, a glossary of terms, and a select bibliography. (ML385.C7)

POPULAR AMERICAN COMPOSERS, FROM REVOLUTIONARY TIMES TO THE PRESENT, 1962, and suppl. 1972, Wilson. Includes some portraits. Mainly represents composers belonging to the past. (ML390.E845)

WHO'S WHO IN MUSIC, 1972, Hafner. Biographies of many celebrated names throughout the world. General articles and a directory of manufacturers, retailers, music societies, and festivals. (ML106.G7W44)

See also: A5—A6.

CHAMBER MUSIC

COBBETT'S CYCLOPEDIC SURVEY OF CHAMBER MUSIC, 2nd ed., 1963, Oxford. (ML1100.C7)

GENERAL WORKS

THE AMERICAN MUSIC HANDBOOK, 1974, Free Press. Covers various organizations, festivals, institutions, suppliers, etc. related to music. (ML13.P39)

CONCISE OXFORD DICTIONARY OF MUSIC, 10th ed., 1970, Oxford. Good but condensed. (ML100.S367)

DICTIONARY OF CONTEMPORARY MUSIC, 1974, Dutton. (ML100.V55)

A DICTIONARY OF MUSICAL TERMS, by T. Baker, 1923, Schirmer. English, French, German, Italian, Latin, and Greek words defined. (ML108.B165)

A DICTIONARY OF MUSICAL THEMES, by H. Barlow, 1948, Crown. Themes of instrumental music arranged by composer. (ML128.I65B3)

A DICTIONARY OF VOCAL THEMES, by H. Barlow, 1950, Crown and Ambassador. Helps to identify and locate a wide variety of vocal themes in standard music. (ML128.V7B3)

GROVE'S DICTIONARY OF MUSIC AND MUSICIANS, 9 vols., 1954, supplement 1961, St. Martin's. Most famous major reference work on music, including biographies, musical terms, and so forth. (ML100.G8863)

HARVARD DICTIONARY OF MUSIC, 2nd ed., 1969, Harvard. Brief entries but a very valuable volume. (ML100.A84)

THE INTERNATIONAL CYCLOPEDIA OF MUSIC AND MUSICIANS, 10th ed., 1974, Dodd. Probably the best one-volume work. (ML100.T47)

THE MUSICIAN'S GUIDE: THE DIRECTORY OF THE WORLD OF MUSIC, 1972, Music Information Service. Covers associations; competitions, awards and grants; education; libraries, publications, and recordings; performance; profession; and trade and industry. (ML13.M505)

THE NEW COLLEGE ENCYCLOPEDIA OF MUSIC, 1960, Norton. Comprehensive. (ML100.W48)

OXFORD COMPANION TO MUSIC, 10th ed., 1970 Oxford. Covers almost every phase of music. (ML100.S37)

THESAURUS OF SCALES AND MELODIC PATTERNS, 1947, Coleman-Ross. Shows the inexhaustible amount of possible scale patterns and their melodic forms. (MT45.S55)

HISTORY

THE NEW OXFORD HISTORY OF MUSIC, 11 vols., 1954–, Oxford. Chronological in organization from ancient to modern music; this is not a revision of the following work but an entirely new work. (ML160.O98)

THE OXFORD HISTORY OF MUSIC, 2nd ed., 8 vols., 1929–1938, Oxford. Important reference history. (ML160.N44)

INDEXES

EDUCATION INDEX, 1929–, Wilson. For educational subjects. (Z5813.E23)

GUIDE TO THE MUSICAL ARTS, 1953–1956, by S.Y. Belknap, 1957, Scarecrow. Lists articles and illustrations. (ML113.B7)

MUSIC INDEX, 1949–, Information Service, Inc. Devoted exclusively to music. Some brief annotations. Good for some biographical information not found elsewhere. (See Card Catalog)

THE NEW YORK TIMES INDEX, 1851–, The New York Times. Good for current information. (AI21.N44)

READERS' GUIDE TO PERIODICAL LITERATURE, 1900–, Wilson. General information. (AI3.R496)

▪B128 OPERA

THE COMPLETE BOOK OF LIGHT OPERA, 1962, Appleton-Century-Crofts. Good source of synopses. (MT95.L85)

CROWELL'S HANDBOOK OF WORLD OPERA, 1961, Crowell. Covers all important operas. (ML102.O6M6)

NEW ENCYCLOPEDIA OF THE OPERA, by D. Ewen, rev. ed., 1971, Hill and Wang. Comprehensive treatment of all opera subjects. (ML102.O6E9)

KOBBE'S COMPLETE OPERA BOOK, rev. 1972, Putnam. The most complete general guide available. (MT95.K52)

See also: B127.

▪B129 ORCHESTRATION

THESAURUS OF ORCHESTRAL DEVICES, by G. Read, 1953, Pitman. Summarizes and lists illustrations of hundreds of orchestral devices. (MT70.R37)

See also: B127.

∎B130   PAINTERS

BRYAN'S DICTIONARY OF PAINTERS AND ENGRAVERS, 5 vols., rev. ed., 1964, Kennikat. Standard biographical work. (N40.B945)

DICTIONARY OF AMERICAN PAINTERS, SCULPTORS AND ENGRAVERS, 1965, Carr. Brief sketches. (N6536.F5)
See also: B117.

∎B131   PAINTING, GENERAL WORKS

CYCLOPEDIA OF PAINTERS AND PAINTING, 4 vols., 1969, Kennikat. Good for older artists. (ND30.C4)

ENCYCLOPEDIA OF PAINTING, by B. Meyers, 3rd ed., 1970, Crown. General articles and biographies of principal painters of all countries and times. (ND30.E5)

ENCYCLOPEDIA OF WORLD ART, 15 vols., 1959−68, McGraw-Hill. Comprehensive guide to world art. (N31.E4833)

PAINTING IN THE TWENTIETH CENTURY, by W. Haftmann, 2 vols., 1960, Praeger. (ND195.H323)
See also: B117.

∎B132   PAINTINGS—REPRODUCTIONS

CATALOGUE OF COLOUR REPRODUCTIONS OF PAINTINGS 1860 TO 1969, 1969 (revised frequently), UNESCO. Gives size, price, and publisher. (ND47.U5)

A GUIDE TO COLOR REPRODUCTIONS, 2nd ed., 1971, Scarecrow. (NE1850.B3)

INDEX TO ART REPRODUCTIONS IN BOOKS, 1974, Scarecrow. Covers outstanding art books published between 1956 and 1971. (N7525.H48)

INDEX TO REPRODUCTIONS OF AMERICAN PAINTINGS, 1948, and supplement, 1964, Wilson. (ND205.M57)

INDEX TO REPRODUCTIONS OF EUROPEAN PAINTINGS, 1956, Wilson. (ND45.M6)
See also: B40a.

∎B133   PHONOGRAPH RECORDS

ANNUAL INDEX TO POPULAR MUSIC RECORD REVIEWS, 1973− (annual), Scarecrow. Covers 35 journals. (ML156.9.A75)

CHICOREL INDEX TO THE SPOKEN ARTS ON DISCS, TAPES, AND CASSETTES, 1973, Chicorel Library. International in scope. (Z5781.C485)

RECORD AND TAPE REVIEWS INDEX, 1971– (annual), Scarecrow. (ML156.9.M28)

SCHWANN CATALOGS, (annual), W. Schwann. Various catalogs are available from record or tape dealers. Covers all currently available records and tapes.

SPOKEN RECORDS, by H. Roach, 3rd ed., 1970, Scarecrow. Contains hundreds of spoken records in English. (Z2011.R6)

THE WORLD'S ENCYCLOPEDIA OF RECORDED MUSIC, 1966 and Suppls., Greenwood. A monumental work concerning all recordings. (ML156.2.C6)

See also: Current periodicals and newspapers.

■ **B134 PHOTOGRAPHY—BIBLIOGRAPHY**

PHOTOGRAPHIC LITERATURE, 1962, Bowker. (Z7134.B6)

RECORDS
See: B133.

■ **B135 SONGS**

SONG INDEX, 1926, supplement 1934, Wilson. Useful for finding the following: words of a wanted song or songs by a given composer, authorship, and whether a song has been translated or is itself a translation, and so forth. (ML128.S353)

SONGS IN COLLECTIONS: AN INDEX, 1966, Information Service, Inc. Augments the SONG INDEX covering collections published between 1940–1957. (ML128.S3D37)

■ **B136 SCULPTURE**

DICTIONARY OF MODERN SCULPTURE, 1962, Tudor. (NB50.D53)

SCULPTURE INDEX, 2 vols., 1970, Scarecrow. Guide to pictures of sculpture. Emphasis on Americas, England, and Europe since 1900. (NB36.C55)

See also: B117.

■ **B137 SPEECH—BIBLIOGRAPHY AND INDEXES**

BIBLIOGRAPHY OF SPEECH AND ALLIED AREAS, 1950–1960, 1962, Chilton. (Z6514.S7M8)

SPEECH INDEX, 1900–1965, and Suppl., 1966–1970, by R.D. Sutton, 1966, Scarecrow. Includes introductions, social and political talks, toasts, and so forth. (AI3.S85)

See also: A4.

TAPES
See: B109, B133.

■ **B138   THEATER**

BIBLIOGRAPHY

CHICOREL BIBLIOGRAPHY TO THE PERFORMING ARTS, 1972, Chicorel Library. (Z5781.C485)

GUIDE TO THE MUSICAL ARTS, by S. Y. Belknap, 1957, Scarecrow. Analytical index of articles and illustrations. (ML113.B37)

PERFORMING ARTS/BOOKS IN PRINT: AN ANNOTATED BIBLIOGRAPHY, 1973, Drama Book Specialists. (Z6935.S34)

THEATRE AND ALLIED ARTS, by B. M. Baker, 1952, Wilson. Annotated. (Z5781.B18)

See also: B180.

BIOGRAPHY

WHO'S WHO IN THE THEATRE, 1912–, Pitman. Besides biographical information, lists of notable productions on the London stage, New York stage, and so forth. (PN2012.W5)

GENERAL WORKS

COMPLETE BOOK OF THE AMERICAN MUSICAL THEATER, by D. Ewen, 1958, Holt. From 1866 to the present, including plot, stars, songs. (ML1711.E9)

THE OXFORD COMPANION TO THE THEATRE, 3rd ed., 1968, Oxford. Covers all phases with emphasis on British and European stage. (PN2035.H3)

SIMON'S DIRECTORY OF THEATRICAL MATERIALS, SERVICES AND INFORMATION (annual), Package Publicity Service. Very comprehensive. (PN2289.S5)

THEATRE BACKSTAGE FROM A TO Z, Rev. ed., 1973, U. of Washington. A dictionary of technical theatre terms. (PN2035.L6)

WHO'S WHO IN THE THEATRE, 1912–, Pitman. Biographical record of the contemporary stage including many listings on the theater. (PN2012.W5)

See also: B180.

B139–B162   HISTORY AND POLITCAL SCIENCE

■ B139   AFRICA

AFRICA, A HANDBOOK TO THE CONTINENT, 1966, Praeger. (DT30.L38)

AFRICA CONTEMPORARY RECORD, ANNUAL SURVEY AND DOCUMENTS, 1969– (annual), Africana. Emphasis is on events of major significance and interest. (DT.L43)

AFRICA SOUTH OF THE SAHARA, (annual), Europa. (DT351.A37)

THE MIDDLE EAST AND NORTH AFRICA, (annual), Europa. (DS49.M5)

See also: B141, B143b, B162.

■ B139a   ANCIENT HISTORY

CAMBRIDGE ANCIENT HISTORY, 1923–1939, 17 vols. (being revised), Cambridge. Covers Assyria, Babylonia, Egypt, Greece, Hittite Empire, Persia, and Rome. Good bibliographies. (D57.C252)

EVERYMAN'S CLASSICAL ATLAS, by J. O. Thomson, 1961, Dent. (G1033.A8)

HARPER'S DICTIONARY OF CLASSICAL LITERATURE AND ANTIQUITIES, 1897, Cooper. Old, but good. (DE5.P36)

OXFORD CLASSICAL DICTIONARY, 2nd ed., 1970, Oxford. Scholarly and comprehensive. (DE5.09)

See also: B140, B176.

■ B139b   ASIA

ASIA: A HANDBOOK, 1965, Praeger. (DS5.W5)

ASIA, A SELECTED AND ANNOTATED GUIDE TO REFERENCE WORKS, 1971, M.I.T. By country. (Z3001.N79)

THE FAR EAST AND AUSTRALASIA, (annual), Europa. (DS1.F3)

See also: B141, B143a, B162.

■ B140   ATLASES

ATLAS OF AMERICAN HISTORY, edited by J. T. Adams, 1943. Scribner. (G1201.S1A2)

ATLAS OF MESOPOTAMIA, 1962, Nelson. (G2251.E6B42)

ATLAS OF THE CLASSICAL WORLD, 1959, Nelson. (DE29.H463)

ATLAS OF WORLD HISTORY, 1965, Rand McNally. (G1030.R3)

GOODE'S WORLD ATLAS, 13th ed., 1970, Rand McNally. (G1019.G67)

HISTORICAL ATLAS, 1964, 9th rev. ed., Barnes & Noble. (G1030.S4)

HAMMOND'S HISTORICAL ATLAS, 1954, C. S. Hammond. (G1030.H32)

MUIR'S HISTORICAL ATLAS, MEDIEVAL AND MODERN, 9th ed., 1963, Barnes & Noble. From Middle Ages on. (G1030.M84)

THE NATIONAL ATLAS OF THE UNITED STATES OF AMERICA, 1970, U.S. Dept. of the Interior. The official national atlas presenting the primary physical, economic, social, and historical features of the country. (G1200.U57)

RAND McNALLY NEW COSMOPOLITAN WORLD ATLAS, 1971, Rand McNally. (G1019.R24)

THE TIMES ATLAS OF THE WORLD, 1955–1959, 5 vols., Houghton. Great in detail. Comprehensive. (G1019.T52)

■B141 BIBLIOGRAPHIES, GENERAL

FOREIGN AFFAIRS BIBLIOGRAPHY, 4 vols., 1919–1962, Harper and Bowker. A useful list selected and annotated. (Z6463.F73)

GUIDE TO HISTORICAL LITERATURE, edited by G. F. Howe, 1961, A.H.A. A selective annotated list. Excellent. (Z6201.A55)

GUIDE TO REFERENCE MATERIALS IN POLITICAL SCIENCE, 1966–, Colorado Bibliographic Institute. Brief, descriptive annotations. (Z7161.W9)

A GUIDE TO THE STUDY OF MEDIEVAL HISTORY, by L. J. Paetow, 1931, Crofts. Probably the most useful general guide. (Z6203.P19)

INTERNATIONAL BIBLIOGRAPHY OF POLITICAL SCIENCE, 1952, (annual), Aldine. Comprehensive. (Z7163.I64)

POLITCAL SCIENCE, A BIBLIOGRAPHICAL GUIDE, 1965 and suppls., Scarecrow. (Z7161.H27)

THE READER'S ADVISER AND BOOKMAN'S MANUAL, edited by H. R. Hoffman, 2 vols., 11th ed., 1968–69, Bowker. A guide to basic books in a variety of fields. Some notes on best editions of a work. (Z1035.B7)

A SELECT BIBLIOGRAPHY: ASIA, AFRICA, EASTERN EUROPE, LATIN AMERICA, 1960, suppl. 1961–1971, 1973, American University Field Staff. Annotated with basic volumes indicated by "A." (Z5579.A512)
See also: B11.

■ B142 BIOGRAPHY

THE HISTORY MAKERS, LEADERS AND STATESMEN OF THE 20th CENTURY, 1973, St. Martin's. (See Card Catalog)
WHO WAS WHEN? A DICTIONARY OF CONTEMPORARIES, 2nd ed., 1950, Wilson. Lists contemporaries of any given important person. (CT103.D4)
WHO'S WHO IN HISTORY, 5 vols., 1960–, Barnes & Noble. A general outline history of Britain, portraits, glossary of terms, and bibliographies. (DA28.W618)
See also: A5–A6, B11a.

■ B143 CANADA

CANADA YEARBOOK, (annual), Information Services Division, Dominion Bureau of Statistics. (HA744.S81)
DICTIONARY OF CANADIAN BIOGRAPHY, 1966–, University of Toronto. (F1005.D5)
HISTORICAL STATISTICS OF CANADA, 1965, Cambridge. (HA746.U7)
McGRAW-HILL DIRECTORY AND ALMANAC OF CANADA, 1966– (annual), McGraw-Hill. Brief but comprehensive coverage. (F1004.7M3)
See also: B141, B143b, B162.

■ B143a CHINA

CHINA: A HANDBOOK, 1973, Praeger. Covers contemporary China. (DS706.W8)
HISTORICAL ATLAS OF CHINA, 1966, Aldine. (G2306.S1H4)
RAND McNALLY ILLUSTRATED ATLAS OF CHINA, 1972, Rand McNally. (G1019.R4.56)
THE TIMES ATLAS OF CHINA, 1974, Harper. Very comprehensive. (See Card Catalog)
See also: B141, B143b, B162.

CITIES
See: B161.

CIVIL WAR
See: B161.

COMMUNISM
See: B155.

CONGRESS
See: B161.

CONSTITUTION OF U.S.
See: B161.

COUNTIES
See: B161.

■**B143b CURRENT INFORMATION**

THE EUROPA YEAR BOOK, 1959– (annual), Europa. Arrangement is alphabetical by country. Up-to-date, accurate, and comprehensive coverage. (D2.E8)
See also: B18, B153.

DATES
See: B19.

■**B144 DICTIONARIES—POLITICAL**

AMERICAN POLITICAL DICTIONARY, 3rd ed., 1972, Holt. (JK9.P55)
AMERICAN POLITICAL TERMS, AN HISTORICAL DICTIONARY, 1962, Wayne State University. (JK9.S65)
THE CRESCENT DICTIONARY OF AMERICAN POLITICS, 1962, Macmillan. (JK9.M2)
DICTIONARY OF AMERICAN POLITICS, 2nd ed., 1968, Barnes & Noble. (JK9.S5)
DICTIONARY OF POLITICS, 1971, Free Press. (D419.L36)

■**B145 DISCOVERIES**

DICTIONARY OF DISCOVERIES, 1968, Greenwood. (G200.L3)
DICTIONARY OF INVENTIONS AND DISCOVERIES, 1969, Philosophical. Very brief information. (T9.C335)
DISCOVERIES AND INVENTIONS OF THE 20th CENTURY, 1966, Dutton. (T20.C82)

■ **B145a DISSERTATIONS**

DISSERTATIONS IN HISTORY, 2 vols., 1972, Kentucky. Covers United States and Canadian Universities, 1873–1970. (Z6021.K8)
See also: B22.

GEOGRAPHICAL INFORMATION
See: B29, B140.

■ **B146 GOVERNMENT OFFICIALS (WORLDWIDE)**

POLITICAL HANDBOOK AND ATLAS OF THE WORLD, 1927– (annual), Harper. Covers data on all countries. Includes name of capital, government officials, latest population, political parties, and so forth. (JK37.P6)

■ **B147 GREAT BRITAIN**

THE CAMBRIDGE HISTORY OF THE BRITISH EMPIRE, 8 vols., 1929–1959, Cambridge University Press. (DA16.C252)
GREAT BRITAIN THE LION AT HOME: A DOCUMENTARY HISTORY OF DOMESTIC POLICY, 1689–1973, 4 vols., 1974, Bowker. Grouped chronologically and thematically in five sections. (See Card Catalog)
HISTORY OF ENGLAND, edited by C. Oman, 8 vols., 1904–1948, Putnam's. (DA30.P76)
OXFORD HISTORY OF ENGLAND, 14 vols., 1934–1963, Oxford. (DA435.C55)

BIBLIOGRAPHY

BIBLIOGRAPHY OF BRITISH HISTORY, 1485–1789, 3 vols., 1928–70, Oxford. A select, classified-subject list. (See Card Catalog)
SOURCES AND LITERATURE OF ENGLISH HISTORY FROM THE EARLIEST TIMES TO ABOUT 1485, by C. Gross, 2nd ed., 1915, Longmans. The best for this period of English history. (Z2061.C87)

STATISTICS

ABSTRACT OF BRITISH HISTORICAL STATISTICS, 1962, Cambridge. (HA1135.M5)
WHITAKER'S ALMANACK, 1869– (annual), Whitaker. (AY754.W5)

GREECE
See: B139, B140, B143b.

INTERNATIONAL HISTORY
See: B143a, B162.

■B148   INTERNATIONAL ORGANIZATIONS

INTERNATIONAL REGIONAL ORGANIZATIONS, 1962, Praeger. (JX1979.L3)
THE INTERNATIONAL YEARBOOK AND STATESMEN'S WHO'S WHO (annual), Burke's Peerage. (JA51.I57)
YEARBOOK OF INTERNATIONAL ORGANIZATIONS (annual), International Publishers. (JX1904.A42)
YEARBOOK OF THE UNITED NATIONS, 1947— (annual), United Nations. (JX1977.A37A4)
See also: A2—A3, B8.

GENERAL HISTORY
See: B143a, B162.

■B148a   JAPAN

HISTORICAL AND GEOGRAPHICAL DICTIONARY OF JAPAN, 1972, Tuttle. A summary of principal events and names occurring in the history and geography of Japan. (PS833.P3)
NIPPON: A CHARTED SURVEY OF JAPAN, (annual), Inter-Culture Associates. Comprehensive, authoritative presentation of contemporary facts. (DS801.N43)
See also: B141, B143b, B162.

■B149   LATIN AMERICA

ENCYCLOPEDIA OF LATIN AMERICA, 1974, McGraw Hill. (F1406.E52)
HANDBOOK OF LATIN AMERICAN STUDIES, 1937— (annual), University of Florida Press. Emphasizes social sciences, humanities, and art. Critical notes are included. (Z1605.H23)

■B150   LEGISLATION, U.S.

CONGRESSIONAL INDEX (annual), Commerce Clearing House, Inc. Loose-leaf service record of the disposition of all bills and resolutions introduced into Congress. (J69.C6)
CONGRESSIONAL QUARTERLY ALMANAC, 1945— (weekly and annual), Congressional Quarterly, Inc. Presents facts on Congress and politics. Complete, concise, and unbiased. (JK1.C66)

U.S. CODE CONGRESSIONAL AND ADMINISTRATIVE NEWS (semi-monthly), West Publishing or E. Thompson Co. Covers President's messages, executive orders, proclamations, congressional and administrative highlights, and so forth. A good steppingstone to the CONGRESSIONAL RECORD. (K.A32)
See also: B161.

MAPS
See: B65, B140.

■B151   MEDIEVAL HISTORY

CAMBRIDGE MEDIEVAL HISTORY, 8 vols., 1911–1936, Cambridge. Good and authoritative. (D118.C3)
A GUIDE TO THE STUDY OF MEDIEVAL HISTORY, by L. J. Paetow, 1931, Crofts. Most useful bibliography. Critical and scholarly. (Z6203.P19)
See also: B153, B162.

■B151a   MIDDLE EAST

THE MIDDLE EAST AND NORTH AFRICA, (annual), Europa. (DS49.M5)
See also: B143b, B162.

■B151b   MILITARY

THE ALMANAC OF WORLD MILITARY POWER, 3rd ed., 1974, Bowker. Information on military and defense apparatus of every country. (UA15.D9)
THE ENCYCLOPEDIA OF MILITARY HISTORY FROM 3500 B.C. TO THE PRESENT, 1970, Harper. Chronologically and geographically arranged. (D25.A2D8).
See also: B161, Wars.

■B152   MODERN HISTORY

NEW CAMBRIDGE MODERN HISTORY, 14 vols., 1958–, Cambridge. (D208.N4)

■B153   PERIODICAL INDEXES

HISTORICAL ABSTRACTS, 1955–, American Bibliographical Center—Elio Press. Useful in extensive research of world, except the U.S. and Canada. (D299.H5)

AMERICA: HISTORY AND LIFE, 1964–, American Bibliographical Center—Clio Press. Guide to periodical literature in U.S. and Canada, Abstracts covering 1965–1968. (Z1236.A48)

THE NEW YORK TIMES INDEX, 1851–, The New York Times. For current history and documents. (AI21.N44)

NINETEENTH CENTURY READER'S GUIDE, 1800–1899, 2 vols., 1944, Wilson. Good for historical subjects but periodicals indexed are largely literary. (AI3.R496)

POOLE'S INDEX TO PERIODICAL LITERATURE, 1802–1907, Smith. Most useful guide to nineteenth-century periodical literature. (AI3.P7)

PUBLIC AFFAIRS INFORMATION SERVICE BULLETIN, 1915–, Public Affairs Information Service. Indexes on a selective basis: periodicals, books, documents. (Z7163.P9)

READER'S GUIDE TO PERIODICAL LITERATURE, 1900–, Wilson. General information. (AI3.R496)

SOCIAL SCIENCES INDEX, 1974, Wilson. Of major importance. Former name was SOCIAL SCIENCES AND HUMANITIES INDEX. (See Card Catalog)

PLACES
See: B29.

■ **B154   POLITICAL PARTIES AND EVENTS**

AMERICAN POLITICAL PARTIES, 1969, Libraries Unlimited. The bibliography is arranged by subject and individual party. Covers movements of the 20th century. (Z165.U5W88)

CONGRESSIONAL QUARTERLY ALMANAC, 1945– (weekly and annual), Congressional Quarterly, Inc. Presents facts on Congress and politics. Complete, concise, and unbiased. (JK1.C66)

POLITICAL RESEARCH, 1973, Basic. Comprehensive and useful to any research in this field. (JA73.L43)

EUROPA YEARBOOK, 1926– (annual), Europa Publications Limited. International in scope, but European emphasis. (D2.E8)

NATIONAL PARTY PLATFORMS, 1840–1964, 1966. University of Illinois. (JK2255.P6)

POLITICAL HANDBOOK AND ATLAS OF THE WORLD, 1927– (annual), Harper. Covers European organizations followed by countries. For each country, gives information on religion, the press, publishers, colleges, and so forth. (JK37.P6)

NATIONAL PARTY PLATFORMS, 1840–1964, 1966, Univ. of
Illinois. (JK2255.P6)

WHO'S WHO IN AMERICAN POLITICS, 1971, (Revised frequently), Bowker. (E176.W6424)

See also: B153, B161.

PRESIDENTS
See: B161.

ROME
See: B139, B140.

■ **B155   RUSSIA**

EVERYMAN'S CONCISE ENCYCLOPEDIA OF RUSSIA, 1961,
Dutton. Covers principal aspects of contemporary Russia and
its historical background. (DK28.U83)

GREAT SOVIET ENCYCLOPEDIA, 30 vols., 3rd ed., 1973–,
Macmillan. Reflects the Soviet's point of view. (AE5.B58)

HANDBOOK OF SOVIET SOCIAL SCIENCE DATA, 1973, Free
Press. Valuable statistical information. (HN523.5.M5)

INFORMATION U.S.S.R., by R. Maxwell, 1962, Pergamon.
Authoritative, including many statistics. (DK14.M38)

McGRAW-HILL ENCYCLOPEDIA OF RUSSIA AND THE
SOVIET UNION, 1961, McGraw-Hill. Comprehensive, cover-
ing every aspect from medieval times to the present.
(DK14.M26)

WORLD COMMUNISM: A HANDBOOK 1918–1965, 1973,
Hoover Institution. The best one volume work on the subject.
(HX40.S89)

YEARBOOK ON INTERNATIONAL COMMUNIST AFFAIRS,
3rd ed., 1971, Hoover Institution. Excellent coverage and
authoritative. (HX1.Y4)

BIBLIOGRAPHY

BASIC RUSSIAN PUBLICATIONS, 1962, University of Chicago.
Annotated. (Z249.H6)

BOOKS ON COMMUNISM, 1963, Amerrand. Covers 1945 through
1962. Selective, annotated list. (Z7164.S67K666)

BOOKS ON SOVIET RUSSIA, 1917–1942, by P. Grierson, 1943,
Saunders. Classified guide, annotated. (Z2510.G75)

THE LITERATURE OF COMMUNISM IN AMERICA, 1962,
Catholic University of America. Lists materials on all aspects

of communism. (Z7164.S7D4)

RUSSIA AND THE SOVIET UNION, A BIBLIOGRAPHIC GUIDE TO WESTERN-LANGUAGE PUBLISHERS, edited by P. L. Horecky, 1965, University of Chicago. (Z2491.H64)

BIOGRAPHY

PROMINENT PERSONALITIES IN THE USSR, 1968–, Scarecrow. A continuation of WHO'S WHO IN THE USSR. (DK275.A1W53)

See also: B143b, B162.

■B156 SOUTH AMERICA

SOUTH AMERICAN HANDBOOK, 1924– (annual), Rand McNally. General information on each country. (F1401.S71)

See also: B149.

■B157 STATE GOVERNMENT

BOOK OF THE STATES, 1935– (biennial), Council of State Government. Comprehensive guide on state activities. (JK2403.B6)

See also: State legislative manuals (titles vary with state and are usually published annually).

■B158 STATISTICS

DEMOGRAPHIC YEARBOOK, 1949– (annual), United Nations. Most authoritative summary of vital statistics of the world. (HA17.D45)

EUROPA YEARBOOK, 1926–, (annual), Europa Publications Limited. International in scope, but European emphasis. (D2.E8)

STATISTICAL YEARBOOK, 1948– (annual), United Nations. Covers most important data in a variety of fields, covering all countries. (HD7293.A49H67)

See also: A2, A3, B153.

■B159 TRAVEL—BIBLIOGRAPHY

A REFERENCE GUIDE TO THE LITERATURE OF TRAVEL, 3 vols., 1935–1949, Greenwood. Lists in chronological order, from the earliest date to 1800. Annotated. (Z6011.C87)

■B160 UNITED NATIONS

A GUIDE TO THE USE OF UNITED NATIONS' DOCUMENTS, by B. Brimmer, 1962, Oceana. Describes various publishing patterns of the United Nations' organizations and suggests research approaches. (Z674.N47)

YEARBOOK OF THE UNITED NATIONS, 1947– (annual), United Nations. Summarizes activities, gives texts of documents, lists publications by or about the United Nations, and includes some biographies. (JX1977.A37A4)

■B161   UNITED STATES
ATLASES
See: B140.

BIBLIOGRAPHIES

THE AMERICAN BIBLIOGRAPHY (1639–1799), by C. Evans, 12 vols., Bowker (Readex Microprint). Most important list of early American publications. Comprehensive. (Z1215.E)

CIVIL WAR BOOKS, A CRITICAL BIBLIOGRAPHY, 2 vols., 1967 –1968, Louisiana State U. (Z1242.N35)

A DICTIONARY OF BOOKS RELATING TO AMERICA, FROM ITS DISCOVERY TO THE PRESENT TIME, by J. Sabin, 29 vols. 1868–1936, Bowker (Readex Microprint). Important and comprehensive. Includes brief information on many of the works. (Z1201.S2)

GUIDE TO HISTORICAL LITERATURE, 1961, Macmillan. Covers the best of historical literature. Annotated. (Z6201.A55)

GUIDE TO PHOTOCOPIED HISTORICAL MATERIALS IN THE UNITED STATES AND CANADA, 1961, Cornell. Useful for those in search of primary source materials. (Z6209.H3)

A GUIDE TO THE STUDY OF THE UNITED STATES OF AMERICA, 1960, U.S. Government Printing Office. Annotated. Detailed author and subject index. (Z1215.U53)

HARVARD GUIDE TO AMERICAN HISTORY, 2 vols., rev. ed., 1974, Harvard. A selective guide to books and articles. (Z1236.H27)

THE LITERATURE OF AMERICAN HISTORY, by J. N. Larned, 1902, Longs College Book Co. Annotated and classified lists. Indicates source material. (Z1263.L3)

WRITINGS ON AMERICAN HISTORY, 1906– (annual). U.S. Government Printing Office. Inclusive list with many descriptive notes and references to critical reviews. (E172.A60)

BIOGRAPHY
BIOGRAPHICAL DIRECTORY OF THE UNITED STATES EXECUTIVE BRANCH, 1774–1971, 1971, Greenwood. (E176.B575)
NOTABLE NAMES IN AMERICAN HISTORY, 1973, White. Brief, but breadth of coverage is excellent. (E176.N89)
See also: B142 and CONGRESS under B161.

CIVIL WAR
THE CIVIL WAR DICTIONARY, by M. Boatner, 1959, McKay. A most valuable volume covering almost everything. (E468.B7)
WAR OF THE REBELLION: A COMPILATION OF THE OFFICIAL RECORDS OF THE UNION AND CONFEDERATE ARMIES, 130 vols., 1880–1901, U.S. War Dept., Washington. The most comprehensive work on the Civil War. (E464.U6)
WEST POINT ATLAS OF THE CIVIL WAR, 1962, Praeger. (G1201.S5U58)

CONGRESS
BIOGRAPHICAL DIRECTORY OF THE AMERICAN CONGRESS, 1774–1961, 1961, U.S. Government Printing Office. Lists all executive officers from the founding of the government. Biographical sketches of all congressmen since 1774. (JK1010.A5)
CONGRESSIONAL QUARTERLY'S GUIDE TO THE CONGRESS OF THE UNITED STATES, ORIGINS, HISTORY, AND PROCEDURE, 1971, Congressional Quarterly Service. Explains how Congress works, its powers, etc. (JK1021.C56)
CONGRESSIONAL RECORD (published while Congress is in session), U.S. Government Printing Office. Daily record of proceedings of Congress. Speeches and debates in full. Text of bills not included, but record of votes is recorded. (J11.R5)
CONGRESSIONAL STAFF DIRECTORY, 1959– (annual), Congressional Staff Directory. (JK1012.C65)
OFFICIAL CONGRESSIONAL DIRECTORY (irregular), 1809–, U.S. Government Printing Office. Biographical sketches of current members of Congress. Lists members of congressional committees, home addresses of members of Congress and often many other facts and names connected with Congress. (JK1011.U52)

U.S. CODE CONGRESSIONAL AND ADMINISTRATIVE
NEWS (semi-monthly), West Publishing Co. or E. Thompson
Co. Covers President's messages, executive orders,
proclamations, congressional and administrative highlights,
and so forth. A good steppingstone to the CONGRESSIONAL
RECORD. (K.A32)
See also: B154.

CONSTITUTIONS

THE CONSTITUTION OF THE UNITED STATES OF
AMERICA, ANALYSIS AND INTERPRETATION, 1953,
U.S. Government Printing Office. A handy, concise guide to
the interpretation of the Constitution. (KF4527.L3)

CONSTITUTIONS OF THE UNITED STATES, NATIONAL
AND STATE, 2 vols., 1962, Columbia. Includes complete,
current texts of the constitutions of the fifty states and of the
United States. A comprehensive subject-matter index to, and
comparative analysis of, the state constitutional texts here
presented is given in the companion volume: INDEX DIGEST
OF STATE CONSTITUTIONS, 2nd ed., 1959, Columbia.
(KF4527.L3)

COUNTIES AND CITIES

THE AMERICAN COUNTIES, by J. N. Kane, 3rd ed., 1972,
Scarecrow. Includes origin of names, historical data, population, and so forth. (E180.K3)

COUNTY AND CITY DATA BOOK, 1967, U.S. Government Printing Office. Gives population figures and many other
statistics. (HA202.A36)

THE MUNICIPAL YEAR BOOK, 1934– (annual), Inter-City
Managers Association. Activities and statistical data of
American cities. (JS344.C5)

NICKNAMES AND SOBRIQUETS OF U.S. CITIES AND
STATES, 2nd ed., 1970, Scarecrow. (E155.K24)

DOCUMENTS

DOCUMENTS OF AMERICAN HISTORY, by H.S. Commager, 2
vols., 8th ed., 1973. (revised frequently), Appleton.
Chronological arrangement of historic documents to the present edition. (E173.C66)

HISTORIC DOCUMENTS, 1972– (annual). Congressional
Quarterly. Covers key documents of the year. Cumulatively
indexed. (E839.5.H57)

ELECTION STATISTICS

AMERICA VOTES, A HANDBOOK OF CONTEMPORARY AMERICAN ELECTION STATISTICS, 1956– (biennial), Congressional Quarterly. (JK1967.A8)

CONGRESSIONAL QUARTERLY ALMANAC, 1945– (weekly and annual), Congressional Quarterly, Inc. Presents facts on Congress and politics, including records of voting. (JK1.C66)

GENERAL WORKS

ALBUM OF AMERICAN HISTORY, 1969, 6 vols., Scribner's. Colonial times through 1917. (E178.A24)

CONCISE DICTIONARY OF AMERICAN HISTORY, by J. T. Adams, 1962, Scribner's. Covers most important material in the following original work. (E174.A45)

CONGRESS AND THE NATION, 1945–1972, 3 vols., 1965–1973, Congressional Quarterly. A review of Government and Politics, giving major legislation, voting, elections, and political activities. (JK1001.C6)

DICTIONARY OF AMERICAN HISTORY, by J. T. Adams, 6 vols., 1940–1963, Scribner's. Very useful and authoritative. (E174.A43)

DICTIONARY OF UNITED STATES HISTORY, by J. F. Jameson, 1971, Gale. (E174.J319)

DOCUMENTS OF AMERICAN HISTORY, by H. S. Commager, 9th ed., 1973, (revised frequently), Appleton. Chronological arrangement of historic documents to the present edition. (E173.C66)

ENCYCLOPEDIA OF AMERICAN FACTS AND DATES, 6th ed., 1972, Crowell. Chronological order divided into four fields of interest in parallel columns. (E174.5.C3)

ENCYCLOPEDIA OF AMERICAN HISTORY, by R. B. Morris, 1970, Harper. Very good treatment. Comprehensive and authoritative. (E174.5.M847)

GOVERNMENTAL GUIDE, (annual). Variety of information, names in the Federal Government. Georgia Robles Boone. (JK6.G6)

HARPER'S ENCYCLOPEDIA OF UNITED STATES HISTORY, 10 vols., 1974, Gale. Generally good. (E174.L92)

LEGALLY AVAILABLE U.S. GOVERNMENT INFORMATION, 2 vols., 1970, Van Nos Reinhold. A guide to government information which does not involve national security. (KF5753.A33)

PAGEANT OF AMERICA, 1925–1929, 15 vols., Yale University. Each volume covers a separate phase of American development. (E178.5.P)
See also: A1-A3.

PRESIDENTS
BOOK OF PRESIDENTS, by Tim Taylor, 1972, Arno. Comprehensive text and indexes. (E176.1T226)
FACTS ABOUT THE PRESIDENTS, by J. N. Kane, 3rd ed., 1974, Wilson. Includes family history, data on elections, highlights, and so forth. (E176.1.K3)
PICTORIAL HISTORY OF AMERICAN PRESIDENTS, by J. Durant, 6th ed., 1973, Barnes. Brief biographies of each President with many illustrations. (E176.D9)

REVOLUTION
ENCYCLOPEDIA OF THE AMERICAN REVOLUTION, 1966, David McKay. Alphabetically arranged. (E208.B68)
PEOPLE AND EVENTS OF THE AMERICAN REVOLUTION, 1974, Bowker. A chronology of significant events, and biographical directory. (E209.D86)

STATISTICS
DIRECTORY OF FEDERAL STATISTICS FOR LOCAL AREAS, 1966, Super. of Documents. Comprehensive finding guide to current sources of Federally published statistics since 1960. (HB2175.A5)
GUIDE TO U.S. GOVERNMENT STATISTICS, 1961, Documents Index. Arranged by departments and agencies with a detailed subject index. (Z7554.U5G8)
HISTORICAL STATISTICS OF THE SOUTH, 1790–1970, 1973, U. of Alabama. Covers sixteen States, population, agriculture, and manufacturing. (HA218.D63)
HISTORICAL STATISTICS OF THE UNITED STATES, COLONIAL TIMES TO 1957, 1960, U.S. Government Printing Office. Covers economic, political, social, and vital statistics. (HA202.A385)
STATISTICAL ABSTRACTS OF THE UNITED STATES, 1878– (annual), U.S. Government Printing Office. Best place to start for gathering any United States statistics. (HA202.)
See also: A2–A3, B46, and Counties and Cities above.

WARS

WEST POINT ATLAS OF AMERICAN WARS, 2 vols., 1959, Praeger. Excellent maps. (G1201.S1U5)

■B162 WORLD HISTORY, GENERAL

CAMBRIDGE ANCIENT HISTORY, 1923-1939, 17 vols., Cambridge. Comprehensive with good bibliographies. (D57.C252)

CAMBRIDGE MEDIEVAL HISTORY, 1911–1936, 8 vols., Cambridge. Good and authoritative. (D117.C3)

ENCYCLOPAEDIA BRITANNICA. 9th ed. 25 vols., and 11th ed., 29 vols., ENCYCLOPAEDIA BRITANNICA. Often of more use than current editions for historical material. (AE5.E36)

AN ENCYCLOPEDIA OF WORLD HISTORY, by W. L. Langer, 5th ed., 1972, Houghton. Very useful, comprehensive, and authoritative. (D21.L27)

HARPER ENCYCLOPEDIA OF THE MODERN WORLD: A CONCISE REFERENCE HISTORY FROM 1760 TO THE PRESENT, 1970, Harper. Arranged chronologically and by topical section. (D205.H35)

NEW CAMBRIDGE MODERN HISTORY, 1958–, 14 vols., Cambridge. Authoritative and comprehensive. (D208.N4)

NEW LARNED HISTORY, 1922–1924, 12 vols., C. A. Nichols. Old but useful. (D9.L32)

ORAL HISTORY COLLECTIONS, 1974, Bowker. List oral history collections located in libraries, oral history centers, and archives. (See Card Catalog)

WORLDMARK ENCYCLOPEDIA OF THE NATIONS, 5 vols., 1971, Worldmark. (G103.W65)

THE YEAR BOOK OF WORLD AFFAIRS, 1947– (annual), Praeger. Covers the principal events and issues of each year. (JX21.Y4)

See also: A1–A3 and specific subjects.

B163–B168 LANGUAGES

■B163 ENGLISH

HARBOSE COLLEGE HANDBOOK, 7th ed., 1972, Harcourt. (PE1112.H6)

A SHORT INTRODUCTION TO ENGLISH USAGE, 1972, McGraw-Hill. (PE1106.L28)

WRITER'S GUIDE AND INDEX TO ENGLISH, 5th ed., 1972,
   Scott, Foresman. (PE1411.P4)
See also: A7.

■B163a FRENCH

GRAND LAROUSSE ENCYCLOPEDIQUE, 10 vols., 1960–1964,
   and Suppl. 1968, LIBRAIRIE LAROUSSE. (AE25.G64)
GRAND ENCYCLOPEDIE, 21 vols., 1972–1976, Librairie
   Larousse. Treats science and technology in the service of man.
   (See Card Catalog)
HARRAP'S STANDARD FRENCH AND ENGLISH
   DICTIONARY, 3 vols., 1972, Scribner's. (PC2640.H3)
THE NEW CASSELL'S FRENCH DICTIONARY, 1970, Funk.
   (PC2640.C3)
NOUVEAU PETIT LAROUSSE, 1972, Larousse and Co. The most
   famous one-volume dictionary-encyclopedia. (AG25.L37)

■B164 GERMAN

A DICTIONARY OF MODERN GERMAN PROSE USAGE, 1961,
   Oxford. (PF3640.E38)
A GERMAN-ENGLISH DICTIONARY OF IDIOMS, 3rd ed., 1969,
   Adler. (PE3460.T3)
DER GROSSE BROCKHAUS, 14 vols., 1952–1963, Adler.
   (AE27.G67)
THE NEW CASSELL'S GERMAN DICTIONARY, 1971, Funk.
   (PF3640.B45)

■B165 LATIN

CASSELL'S NEW LATIN DICTIONARY, 1959, Funk.
   (PA2365.L3C3)
SMALLER LATIN-ENGLISH DICTIONARY, 3rd rev. ed., 1962,
   Barnes & Noble. (PA2365.E5S6)

■B166 RUSSIAN

THE OXFORD RUSSIAN-ENGLISH DICTIONARY, 1972, Ox-
   ford. (PG2640.W5)
RUSSIAN-ENGLISH DICTIONARY, 7th ed., 1967, Dutton.
   (PG2640.S5)

■B167 SPANISH

APPLETON'S NEW CUYOS DICTIONARY, 5th ed., rev., 1972,

Appleton. (PC4640.C8)

CASSELL'S BEYOND THE DICTIONARY IN SPANISH, 2nd ed., 1972, Funk. Bridges the gap between the written word and speech. (PC4445.G4)

CASSELL'S SPANISH DICTIONARY, 1966, Funk. (PC464.C35)

ENCYCLOPEDIA UNIVERSAL ILUSTRADA EUROPEO-AMERICANA, 97 vols., 1933, suplemento and apendice vols. also, Madrid, Espana. (DP17.E5)

NEW REVISED VALAZQUEZ SPANISH AND ENGLISH DICTIONARY, 1967, Follett. (See Card Catalog)

B168　PUBLICATIONS IN FOREIGN LANGUAGES

AYER'S DIRECTORY OF NEWSPAPERS AND PERIODICALS, 1880– (annual), Ayer. (Z6951.A97)

B169–B195　LITERATURE

■**B169　AMERICAN LITERATURE, GENERAL INFORMATION**

CAMBRIDGE HISTORY OF AMERICAN LITERATURE, 4 vols., 1917–1921, Cambridge. A standard and important work; Colonial times to early twentieth century. (PS88.C3)

CONCISE DICTIONARY OF AMERICAN LITERATURE, by R. L. Richards, 1959, Littlefield. (PS21.R5)

LITERARY HISTORY OF THE UNITED STATES, 3rd ed., 2 vols., 1963, and Suppl. 1972, Macmillan. A comprehensive history from Colonial times to 1961. (PS88.L522)

OXFORD COMPANION TO AMERICAN LITERATURE, 4th ed., 1965, Oxford. Includes biographies, bibliographies, summaries, and descriptions of major works and periods. (PS21.H3)

THE PENGUIN COMPANION TO AMERICAN LITERATURE, 1971, McGraw-Hill. Covers both North America and Latin America. (PN843.P4)

READER'S ENCYLOPEDIA OF AMERICAN LITERATURE, 1962, Crowell. Covers both American and Canadian literature. Includes biographical data, list of works, and brief plot summary. (PS21.R4)

See also: A1, B186, B187.

■**B170　ANONYMOUS AND PSEUDONYMOUS BOOK INFORMATION**

DICTIONARY OF ANONYMOUS AND PSEUDONYMOUS ENGLISH LITERATURE, 7 vols., 1926–1934, Vol. 8, 1956, Vol. 9, 1926, Oliver and Boyd. Listed by title with the best opinion as to authorship indicated. (Z1065.H17)

HANDBOOK OF PSEUDONYMS AND PERSONAL NICKNAMES, 2 vols., 1972, Scarecrow. (Z1041.S43)

■B171 AUTHORS

BIOGRAPHICAL INFORMATION

AMERICAN AUTHORS 1600–1900, by S. J. Kunitz, 1938, Wilson. Fairly detailed biographies with many portraits. (PS21.KS)

AMERICAN AUTHORS AND BOOKS, 1640–Present, by W. J. Burke, 3rd rev. ed., 1972, Crown. Comprehensive but brief. From the best known authors and books to the least known. (Z1224.B87)

AMERICAN WRITERS: A COLLECTION OF LITERARY BIOGRAPHIES, 4 vols., 1974, Scribner's. Biographical and critical comments, comparisons with other authors, and interpretations. (See Card Catalog)

BRITISH AUTHORS BEFORE 1800, by S. J. Kunitz, 1952, Wilson. Some detailed biographies with some portraits. (PR105.K4)

BRITISH AUTHORS OF THE NINETEENTH CENTURY, by S. J. Kunitz, 1936, Wilson. Some detailed biographies with portraits. (PR451.K8)

COLUMBIA DICTIONARY OF MODERN EUROPEAN LITERATURE, by H. Smith, 1947, Columbia. Concentrates on the author's work, and his contributions and influence. (PN41.C6)

CONTEMPORARY AMERICAN AUTHORS, by F. B. Millett, 1940, Harcourt. Brief sketches with bibliographies of their works. (PS221.M5)

CONTEMPORARY AUTHORS, 1962– (annually), Gale. Brief information; inclusive list. (Z1224.C6)

CONTEMPORARY NOVELISTS, 1972, St. Martin's. (PR737.V5)

A CRITICAL DICTIONARY OF ENGLISH LITERATURE AND BRITISH AND AMERICAN AUTHORS, by S. A. Allibone, 3 vols., and supplement (2 vols.), 1965 (reprint), Gale Research. Brief sketches with bibliographies of author's major works. (Z2010.A44)

CYCLOPEDIA OF WORLD AUTHORS, 2 vols., 1958, Salem.

Covers facts about each author's philosophy and style as well as his life. Bibliographies. (PN41.M26)

ESSAY AND GENERAL LITERATURE INDEX, 1900–, Wilson. Includes listings about authors. (AI3.E752)

EUROPEAN AUTHORS: 1000–1900, 1967, Wilson. (PN451.K8)

INDEX TO LITERARY BIOGRAPHY, 2 vols., 1974, Scarecrow. Covers location of information on some 60,000 authors from antiquity to the present. (See Card Catalog)

TWENTIETH CENTURY AUTHORS, 1942, supplement 1956, Wilson. Outstanding sketches and many portraits. Always consult both volumes. (PN771.K86)

See also: A5–A6, B186.

WORKS, CRITICISMS OF

THE AMERICAN NOVEL, 1789–1959, A CHECKLIST OF TWENTIETH-CENTURY CRITICISM, 1961, and vol. 2, 1960–1968, 1969, Swallow. (Z1231.F4G4)

AUTHORS: CRITICAL AND BIOGRAPHICAL REFERENCES, A GUIDE TO 4,700 CRITICAL AND BIOGRAPHICAL PASSAGES IN BOOKS, 2 vols., 1971, Scarecrow. (PN524.C58)

BOOK REVIEW DIGEST, 1905–, Wilson. (Z1219.C95)

CONTEMPORARY LITERARY CRITICISM: EXCERPTS FROM CRITICISM OF THE WORKS OF TODAY'S NOVELISTS, POETS, PLAYWRIGHTS, AND OTHER CREATIVE WRITERS, 1973–, Gale. Emphasis is on writers in English. (PN771.C59)

A GUIDE TO CRITICAL REVIEWS OF UNITED STATES FICTION, 1870–1910, 2 vols., 1971, 1974, Scarecrow. covers both major and minor U.S. writers. (Z1225.E35)

EIGHT AMERICAN AUTHORS: A REVIEW OF RESEARCH AND CRITICISM, rev. ed., 1972, Norton. Bibliographical essays. Excellent. (PS201.E4)

THE ENGLISH NOVEL, 1578–1956, A CHECKLIST OF TWENTIETH-CENTURY CRITICISM, 1958, Swallow. (Z2014.F4B4)

ESSAY AND GENERAL LITERATURE INDEX, 1900–, Wilson. Excellent guide to criticisms of authors and individual works. (AI3.E752)

A LIBRARY OF LITERARY CRITICISM, MODERN AMERICAN LITERATURE, by D. Nyren, 1960, Ungar. Covers twentieth-century authors. (PS221.N9)

A LIBRARY OF LITERARY CRITICISM, MODERN BRITISH AUTHORS, 3 vols., 1965, Ungar. Covers twentieth-century authors. (PR473.T4)

LIBRARY OF LITERARY CRITICISM OF ENGLISH AND AMERICAN AUTHORS, by C. Moulton, 8 vols., 1901–1905, Smith. Gives brief biographical data followed by selected quotations from criticisms of the author's works. Extracts are lengthy and exact references are given including many classics. (PR83.M73)

SHORT FICTION CRITICISM 1800–1950, 1960, Swallow. Covers short stories and novelettes. (Z5917.S5T5)

See also: B12.

■B172 AUTOBIOGRAPHIES—BIBLIOGRAPHY

A BIBLIOGRAPHY OF AMERICAN AUTOBIOGRAPHIES, by L. Kaplan, 1961, University of Wisconsin. Annotated with location of copies in libraries. (Z1224.K3)

BRITISH AUTOBIOGRAPHIES, 1968, Shoe String. An annotated list covering those works published before 1951. (Z2027.A9M3)

THE READER'S ADVISER AND BOOKMAN'S MANUAL, 2 vols., 11th ed., 1968–1969, Bowker. Selective lists with some notes. (Z1035.B7)

■B173 BIBLIOGRAPHIES, GENERAL

BASIC TOOLS OF RESEARCH: AN ANNOTATED GUIDE FOR STUDENTS OF ENGLISH, 1968, Barron's. (Z2011.V48)

BIBLIOGRAPHICAL GUIDE TO THE STUDY OF THE LITERATURE OF THE U.S.A., 3rd ed., 1970, Duke University. Selective list with good annotations. (Z1225.G6)

BIBLIOGRAPHY OF AMERICAN LITERATURE, by J. Blank, 6 vols. published so far, 1955–, Yale. A selective annotated list. With each author listing is a bibliography of works about him. (Z1225.B55)

BIBLIOGRAPHY OF BIBLIOGRAPHIES IN AMERICAN LITERATURE, 1970, Bowker. Arranged under headings: bibliography, authors, genres, and special subjects. (Z1225.A1N5)

CAMBRIDGE BIBLIOGRAPHY OF ENGLISH LITERATURE, 5 vols, 1941, and supplements, Cambridge. Comprehensive and authoritative, including notes. (Z2011.B28)

A CONCISE BIBLIOGRAPHY FOR STUDENTS OF ENGLISH, 5th ed., 1972, Stanford. Covers both English and American literature. (Z2011.K35)

CONCISE CAMBRIDGE BIBLIOGRAPHY OF ENGLISH LITERATURE, 2nd ed., 1965, Cambridge. Covers four hundred major authors selected from the Cambridge Bibliography of English Literature. (Z2011.W3)

FICTION CATALOG, 8th ed., 1971, and suppls., Wilson. Annotated. (Z5916.W74)

GUIDE TO AMERICAN LITERATURE AND ITS BACKGROUNDS SINCE 1890, 1964, Harvard. (Z1225.J65)

LITERARY HISTORY OF THE UNITED STATES, 3rd ed., 2 vols., 1963, Macmillan. Volume 2 has the bibliographies. (PS88.L522)

MLA INTERNATIONAL BIBLIOGRAPHY, 1921– (annual), New York University. Classified. Very useful. (Z7006.M64)

THE NEW CAMBRIDGE BIBLIOGRAPHY OF ENGLISH LITERATURE, 5 vols., rev. ed., 1971–, Cambridge. An indispensable comprehensive and authoritative classified guide. (Z2011.N45)

READER'S ADVISOR AND BOOKMAN'S MANUAL, 2 vols., 11th ed., 1968–1969, Bowker. By general subjects with notes. (Z1035.B7)

A REFERENCE GUIDE TO ENGLISH STUDIES, by B. F. Bond, 2nd ed., 1970, Chicago. Restricted to the best in each field. (Z1002.B72)

SELECTIVE BIBLIOGRAPHY FOR THE STUDY OF ENGLISH AND AMERICAN LITERATURE, by R. D. Altick, 4th ed., 1971, Macmillan. (Z2011.A4)

YEAR'S WORK IN ENGLISH STUDIES, 1919–, English Association. Grouped by periods, selective and critical comments. (PE58.E6)

See also: B11, B184.

BIOGRAPHY
See: A5–A6, B171.

■ **B174 BIOGRAPHY—BIBLIOGRAPHIES**

THE READER'S ADVISOR AND BOOKMAN'S MANUAL, 2 vols., 11th ed., 1968–1969, (revised frequently), Bowker. Selective with some notes on editions. (Z1035.B7)
See also: B173.

BOOK REVIEWS
See: B12, B171.

▪ B174a CANADIAN LITERATURE

THE OXFORD COMPANION TO CANADIAN HISTORY AND
LITERATURE, 1967, Oxford. A good one-source place to
start. (PR9106.S7)

▪ B175 CHILDREN

LITERATURE

CHILDREN'S CATALOG, 12th ed., 1971, and supplements,
Wilson. Annotated guide, especially to books but including
pamphlets. (Z1037.W76)

EDUCATION INDEX, 1929–, Wilson. (Z5813.E23)

See also: B89, B186.

PLAYS

INDEX TO CHILDREN'S PLAYS IN COLLECTIONS, 1972,
Scarecrow. (PN1627.K7)

SUBJECT INDEX TO CHILDREN'S PLAYS, 1940, American
Library Association. Listed by subject for children up to the
eighth grade. (Z5784.C5A5)

POETRY

CHILDREN'S POETRY INDEX, 1938, Faxon. Poems from
anthologies. (PN1023.M25)

INDEX TO CHILDREN'S POETRY, 1942, supplement 1954, 2nd
supplement 1965, Wilson. Guide to collections of children's
literature. (PN1023.B7)

INDEX TO POETRY FOR CHILDREN AND YOUNG PEOPLE
1964–1969, 1972, Wilson. An extension of the three previous
volumes. (PN1023.B72)

SUBJECT INDEX TO POETRY FOR CHILDREN AND YOUNG
PEOPLE, 1957, American Library Association. Graded from
kindergarten to grade 12. (PN1023.A5)

See also: B191.

▪ B176 CLASSICAL LITERATURE

ATLAS OF THE CLASSICAL WORLD, 1959, Nelson.
(DE29.H463)

CONCISE DICTIONARY OF GREEK LITERATURE, 1962,
Philosophical Library. (DE29.H463)

GREEK AND ROMAN AUTHORS: A CHECKLIST OF
CRITICISM, 1973, Scarecrow. Includes only items written in
English. A comprehensive bibliography. (Z7016.G9)

HARPER'S DICTIONARY OF CLASSICAL LITERATURE AND
ANTIQUITIES, 1897, Cooper. Old work but very good.
(DE5.P36)
NEW CENTURY CLASSICAL HANDBOOK, edited by C. D.
Avery, 1962, Appleton. (DE5.N4)
NEW CENTURY CYCLOPEDIA OF NAMES, edited by C. L.
Barnhart, 3 vols., 1954, Appleton. Includes names and places
of legend and mythology. (PE1625.C43)
OXFORD CLASSICAL DICTIONARY, 2nd ed., 1970, Oxford.
Describes gods, heroes, people, places, myths, and legends of
classical Greece and Rome. (DE5.09)
OXFORD COMPANION TO CLASSICAL LITERATURE, 1937,
Oxford. Comprehensive and scholarly. (DE5.H3)
SHORTER ATLAS OF THE CLASSICAL WORLD, 1962, Harper.
(DE29.S393)
See also: B186.

■B177 COSTUME

BIBLIOGRAPHY
BIBLIOGRAPHY OF COSTUME, by H. Hiler, 1939, Continental.
(Z5691.H64)
COSTUME INDEX, 1937, supplement 1957, Wilson. Comprehen-
sive and detailed, covering almost any period or country.
Illustrations are specifically noted. (Z691.M75)

DICTIONARIES
THE DICTIONARY OF COSTUME, 1969, Scribners. Alphabetical
entries describing articles from various time periods.
(GT507.W5)
A DICTIONARY OF ENGLISH COSTUME, 1960, Adam and
Black. (GT507.C8)

PICTORIAL WORKS
MEDIEVAL COSTUME, ARMOUR AND WEAPONS,
1350−1450, by E. Wagner, 1958, Paul Hamlyn. (GT575.W293)
A PICTORIAL HISTORY OF COSTUME, by W. Bruhn, 1955,
Praeger. From ancient times to the present. (GT513.B763)
TWO CENTURIES OF COSTUME IN AMERICA 1620−1820, 2
vols., 1970 (repr.), Dover. (GT607.E23)

CRITICISMS OF AUTHORS AND THEIR WORKS
See: B171.

■ B178 DIARIES—BIBLIOGRAPHY

AMERICAN DIARIES, by W. Matthews, 1959, Channer. Annotated list prior to the year 1861. (B5305.U5M3)

DICTIONARIES
See: A7.

■ B179 DISSERTATIONS AND THESES IN LITERATURE

DISSERTATIONS IN AMERICAN LITERATURE 1891–1966, 1968, Duke University. (Z1225.W8)

DISSERTATIONS IN ENGLISH AND AMERICAN LITERATURE, 1968, Suppl. 1969, Bowker. (Z5053.M32)

THESES IN ENGLISH LITERATURE 1894–1970, 1973–, Pierian Press. (See Card Catalog)
See also: B22.

■ B180 DRAMA

BIBLIOGRAPHY

BIBLIOGRAPHY OF SPEECH AND ALLIED AREAS, 1970 (repr.) Greenwood. Selective. (Z6514.S7M8)

GUIDE TO REFERENCE AND BIBLIOGRAPHY FOR THEATRE RESEARCH, 1971, Ohio St. U. (Z5781.L87)

THE READER'S ADVISER AND BOOKMAN'S MANUAL, 2 vols., 11th ed., 1968–1969, Selective list with notes. (Z1035.B7)
See also: B173 and below.

GENERAL WORKS

BEST PLAYS OF 19—, 1899– (annual), Dodd. Selected best new American plays of each year with additional information. (PN6112.B45)

CROWELL'S HANDBOOK OF CONTEMPORARY DRAMA, 1971, Crowell. Emphasis is on written drama rather than the theater. (PN1861.C7)

GUIDE TO GREAT PLAYS, by J. T. Shipley, 1956, Public Affairs. Summary of great plays of all periods with some additional information on each. (PN6112.5.S45)

A HANDBOOK OF CLASSICAL DRAMA, by P. W. Harsh, 1944, Stanford. Includes Greek tragedy, old comedy, new comedy, Roman comedy, and Roman tragedy. (PZ3024.H3)

HISTORY OF ENGLISH DRAMA, 1660–1900, 6 vols., 1959, Cambridge. Gives history and other useful material. (PN625.N52)

MASTERS OF MODERN DRAMA, by H. M. Block, 1962, Random. Great plays of the contemporary theater. (PN6112.B48)

McGRAW-HILL ENCYCLOPEDIA OF WORLD DRAMA, 4 vols., 1972, McGraw-Hill. From the beginning of drama, focuses on major dramatists, emphasis is on European tradition. (PN1625.M3)

MODERN WORLD DRAMA: AN ENCYCLOPEDIA, 1972, Dutton. Comprehensive coverage of 20th Century drama. (PN1851.M36)

THE NEW THEATRE HANDBOOK AND DIGEST OF PLAYS, by B. Sobel, 1948, Crown. Brief data on famous plays. (PN1625.S6)

THE OXFORD COMPANION TO THE THEATRE, 3rd ed., 1968, Oxford. Covers all periods of history. Emphasis is on the popular theater. (PN2035.H3)

THE READERS ENCYCLOPEDIA OF WORLD DRAMA, 1969, Crowell. Extensive coverage of drama as literature. (PN1625.G3)

THEATRE LANGUAGE, by W. P. Bowman, 1961. Theatre Arts Books. (PN2035.B6)

See also: A1, B138, B186.

INDEXES

CHICOREL THEATER INDEX TO PLAYS IN COLLECTIONS, ANTHOLOGIES, PERIODICALS, DISCS AND TAPES, 3 vols., 1970−1972, Chicorel. Comprehensive and one of the best indexes. (Z5781.C485)

THE DRAMATIC INDEX, 1909−1949, 39 vols., 1910−1950, Faxon. By subject covering all United States and British periodicals of this period. (Z1007.B94)

INDEX TO FULL-LENGTH PLAYS, 1926−1944, 1946, and supplement 1895−1925, 1956, and 1945−1964, 1965, Faxon. (Z5781.T52)

INDEX TO ONE-ACT PLAYS, 1900−1924, 1924, supplements to 1966, Faxon. Includes types, setting, number of characters by sexes, and so forth. (Z5781.L83)

INDEX TO PLAYS 1800−1926, by I. T. E. Firkin, 1927, supplement 1935, Wilson. Indicates where plays may be found. Partially supplemented by PLAY INDEX. (Z5781.A1F5)

INDEX TO PLAYS IN PERIODICALS, 1971 and suppl. 1973, Scarecrow. (Z5781.K43)

INDEX TO THE BEST PLAYS SERIES 1899–1950, 1950, supplement 1949–1960, 1961, Dodd. This indexes the collections of BEST PLAYS OF 19—, formerly called BURNS MANTLE BEST PLAYS OF 19—. (PN6112.B45)

OTTEMILLER'S INDEX TO PLAYS IN COLLECTIONS, 5th ed., 1971, Scarecrow. Covers 1900–mid-1970. (Z5781.08)

PLAY INDEX: 1949–1952, 1953; 1953–1960, 1963; 1961–1967, 1969; 1968–1972, 1973, Wilson. Annotated with a cast analysis. (Z5781.P53)

READERS' GUIDE TO PERIODICAL LITERATURE, 1905–, Wilson. Look under Drama. (AI3.R496)

See also: B187.

SUMMARIES AND CRITICISM

AMERICAN DRAMA CRITICISM, 1967 and suppl. 1970, Archon. (Z1231.D7P3)

A DIGEST OF 500 PLAYS, edited by T. J. Shank, 1963. Crowell-Collier. World's most significant plays, from ancient Greek drama to modern-day Broadway productions. (PN6112.5.S42)

DIGESTS OF GREAT AMERICAN PLAYS, by J. Lovell, 1961, Crowell. Summaries of more than one hundred plays from 1766–1959. (PS338.P5L6)

DRAMA CRITICISM, 2 vols., 1966–1971, Swallow. (Z1231.D7C6)

DRAMATIC CRITICISM INDEX, 1972, Gale. Selective covering books and periodicals. (Z5781.B8)

EUROPEAN DRAMA CRITICISM, 1968 and suppl. 1970, Shoe String. (Z5781.P2)

A GUIDE TO CRITICAL REVIEWS, 5 vols., 2nd ed., 1973–, Scarecrow. Good source of contemporary drama criticism. (Z5782.S34)

GUIDE TO GREAT PLAYS, by J. T. Shipley, 1956, Public Affairs Press. Gives brief history, background, plot of and original reaction to plays. (PN6112.5.S45)

MASTERPLOTS (annual), Salem. Plot summaries. (PN44.M33A5)

MODERN DRAMA, A CHECKLIST OF CRITICAL LITERATURE ON 20TH CENTURY PLAYS, 1967, Scarecrow. Selective. (Z5781.A35)

THE NEW THEATRE HANDBOOK AND DIGEST OF PLAYS, by B. Sobel, 1948, Crown. Brief data on famous plays. (PN1625.S6)

■B181 DRAMATIC READINGS

INDEX TO DRAMATIC READINGS, 1971 (repr.), Scholarly. (PN4205.S5)

■B182 DRAMATISTS—BIOGRAPHY

BIOGRAPHICAL CHRONICLE OF ENGLISH DRAMA, 1559–1642, 1891, Reeves. Biographical data and list of plays in order of original production. (PR651.F5)
CONTEMPORARY DRAMATISTS, 1973, St. Martin's. (See Card Catalog)
WHO'S WHO IN THE THEATRE, 1912– (not annual), Pitman. Contemporary stage figures. Emphasis on London stage but includes American actors. Bibliographies. (PN2012.W5)
See also: A5–A6.

■B183 ENGLISH LITERATURE

CAMBRIDGE HISTORY OF ENGLISH LITERATURE, 15 vols., 1907–1927, Cambridge. Comprehensive, beginnings to 1900. Authoritative, including bibliographies. (PR83.C22)
THE CONCISE CAMBRIDGE HISTORY OF ENGLISH LITERATURE, 3rd ed., 1970, Cambridge. (PR85.S34)
NEW CENTURY HANDBOOK OF ENGLISH LITERATURE, by C. L. Barnhart, 2nd ed., 1967, Appleton. Covers writers, works of literature in all forms, and literary characters. (PR19.N4)
OXFORD COMPANION TO ENGLISH LITERATURE, 4th ed., 1967, Oxford. Brief, covering authors, books, literary form, and such. Bibliographies. (PR19.H3)
OXFORD HISTORY OF ENGLISH LITERATURE, 12 vols., 1945–, Oxford. Covers beginnings to present. Authoritative, including bibliographies. (PR641.W58)
THE PENGUIN COMPANION TO ENGLISH LITERATURE, 1971, McGraw-Hill. From Saxon times to the present including figures outside the strictly literary field. (PN849.C5P4)
See also: B186, B187.

FABLES
See: B187.

FAIRY TALES
See: B187.

■B184 FICTION—BIBLIOGRAPHY

AMERICAN HISTORICAL FICTION, 3rd ed., 1971, Scarecrow. Classified into chronological periods from Colonial days to the Space Age. Annotations. (PS374.H5D5)

THE CONTEMPORARY NOVEL: A CHECKLIST OF CRITICAL LITERATURE ON THE BRITISH AND AMERICAN NOVELS SINCE 1945, 1972, Scarecrow. Selective. (Z1231.F4)

FICTION CATALOG, 8th ed., 1971, Wilson. Annotations and good subject index. (Z5916.W74)

FICTION INDEX, by G. B. Cotton, 1953, Association of Assistant Librarians. Covers 1945 through 1952. Includes short story collections, anthologies, and omnibus volumes. (Z5916.C78)

GUIDE TO HISTORICAL FICTION, by E. A. Baker, 1969 (repr.), B. Franklin. Mostly novels that portray historical events. Annotated. (Z5917.H6B2)

GUIDE TO HISTORICAL FICTION, by Leonard B. Irwin, 10th ed., 1971, McKinley. Arranged by broad subject categories, with author and title indexes. (Z5917.H617)

GUIDE TO THE BEST FICTION, ENGLISH AND AMERICAN, by E. A. Baker, 1932, Macmillan. Selective. Annotated list. (Z5916.B18)

WORLD'S BEST BOOKS, HOMER TO HEMINGWAY, 1953, Wilson. From 1050 B.C. to A.D. 1950. (Z1035.D555)

See also: B171, B194.

■B185 FRENCH LITERATURE

OXFORD COMPANION TO FRENCH LITERATURE, 1959, Oxford. Covers authors and specific works. (PQ41.H3)

■B186 GENERAL WORKS

BREWER'S DICTIONARY OF PHRASE AND FABLE, 13th rev. ed., 1972, Harper. Useful for odd items connected with literature and mythology. Brief treatment. (PN43.B65)

CASSELL'S ENCYCLOPEDIA OF WORLD LITERATURE, 1973 (repr.) Morrow. General articles and biographies. Brief treatment. (PN41.C3)

COLUMBIA DICTIONARY OF MODERN EUROPEAN LITERATURE, 1947, Columbia. Articles on the modern literature of each European country. Brief biographies and comments on their works. (PN41.C6)

THE CONCISE ENCYCLOPEDIA OF MODERN WORLD
LITERATURE, edited by G. Grigson, 1971, Hawthorn.
Describes the growth of the major national literatures and the
characteristic literary forms of our time. (PN41.C64)

DICTIONARY OF FICTIONAL CHARACTERS, 1963, Writer.
Includes names from novels, short stories, poems, plays, and
operas written in the English language. (PR19.F7)

DICTIONARY OF WORLD LITERATURE, by J. T. Shipley, rev.
ed., 1968, Littlefield. Philosophical Library. Brief entries but
includes many bibliographies. (PN41.S5)

ENCYCLOPEDIA OF WORLD LITERATURE IN THE 20TH
CENTURY, 3 vols., 1967–1971, Ungar. Well documented,
plus bibliography of most important works on a subject.
(PN774.L433)

FUNK & WAGNALLS GUIDE TO MODERN WORLD
LITERATURE, 1973, F & W. (PN761.S43)

A HANDBOOK TO LITERATURE, 3rd ed., 1972, Odyssey.
(PN41.H6)

LONGMAN COMPANION TO TWENTIETH CENTURY
LITERATURE, 1973, Longman. (PN771.W28)

THE PENGUIN COMPANION TO CLASSICAL, ORIENTAL,
AND AFRICAN LITERATURE, 1971, McGraw–Hill. Useful
bibliographies. (PA31.P4)

THE PENGUIN COMPANION TO EUROPEAN LITERATURE,
1971, McGraw–Hill. Includes an index of authors, classified
by language and by country. (PN41.P43)

WORLD LITERATURE SINCE 1945, 1973, Ungar. Complements
ENCYCLOPEDIA OF WORLD LITERATURE IN THE 20th
CENTURY. (PN771.I9)

THE READER'S ENCYCLOPEDIA, 2nd ed., 1965, Crowell.
Covers literary works, forms, types, allusions, and
biographies. (PN41.B4)

See also: A1.

■B187 INDEXES

ESSAYS AND GENERAL LITERATURE INDEX, 1900–,
Wilson. Indexes collections and anthologies that have
appeared in book form. Also useful for lists of essays by a given
author, material on a given subject, biographies, and
criticisms of writers and their books. Excellent for literature.
(AI3.E752)

HUMANITIES INDEX, 1974–, Wilson. Former SOCIAL
SCIENCES AND HUMANITIES INDEX. (See Card
Catalog)
INDEX TO FAIRY TALES, MYTHS, AND LEGENDS, 1926,
supplements 1937, 1952, and 1973, Faxon. Indexes a large
number of collections. Helpful to children's workers.
(Z5983.F17E2)
INDEX TO LITTLE MAGAZINES, 1943–1969, 1972. Swallow.
(AI3.I54)
LIBRARY LITERATURE, 1934, Wilson. (Z666.L69)
NINETEENTH CENTURY READER'S GUIDE TO
PERIODICALS, 1800–1899, 2 vols., 1940, Wilson. (AI3.R496)
POOLE'S INDEX TO PERIODICAL LITERATURE, 1802-1907, 7
vols., 1938, Peter Smith. (AI3.P7)
READER'S GUIDE TO PERIODICAL LITERATURE, 1905- ,
Wilson. (AI3.R496)
SOCIAL SCIENCES AND HUMANITIES INDEX, 1907–1974,
Wilson. Covers the more scholarly journals in the humanities.
Excellent for literature. (AI3.R49)

■B188 LITERARY TERMS

A DICTIONARY OF LITERARY TERMS, 1960, Little. (PN43.D8)
DICTIONARY OF WORLD LITERARY TERMS: FORMS,
TECHNIQUE, CRITICISM, 1970, Writer. (PN41.S5)
A GLOSSARY OF LITERARY TERMS, 3rd ed., 1971, Holt.
(PN445.A2)
READER'S GUIDE TO LITERARY TERMS, 1960, Noonday.
(PN41.B33)
See also: B186.

■B189 NURSERY RHYMES

THE OXFORD DICTIONARY OF NURSERY RHYMES, 1951,
Oxford. Comprehensive and authoritative. (PZ8.3.O60X)

■B190 PHRASES AND ALLUSIONS

BREWER'S DICTIONARY OF PHRASE AND FABLE, 13th rev.
ed., 1972, Harper. Brief treatment. (PN43.B65)

PLAYS
See: B180.

■B191   POETRY

THE CONCISE ENCYCLOPEDIA OF ENGLISH AND AMERICAN POETS AND POETRY, by S. Spender, 1963, Hawthorn. (PR19.S6)

CONTEMPORARY POETS OF THE ENGLISH LANGUAGE, 1971, St. Martin's. (Z2014.P7C63)

ENCYCLOPEDIA OF POETRY AND POETICS, 1972, Princeton. (PN1021.E5)

THE EXPLICATOR CYCLOPEDIA, 1966–, Quadrangle Books. A comprehensive selection of essays which explicate notable British and American poems. (PR401.E9)

GRANGER'S INDEX TO POETRY, 6th ed., 1973, Columbia. Very useful. Listed by title, author, and first line. Subject index. (PN1021.G7)

MASTERPLOTS (annual), Salem. (PN44.M33A5)

POETRY EXPLICATION, A CHECKLIST OF INTERPRETATION SINCE 1925 OF BRITISH AND AMERICAN POEMS, PAST AND PRESENT, by J. M. Kuntz, rev. ed., 1962, Allan Swallow. Comprehensive index of poetry explications printed during the period 1925-1959. Very useful. (Z2014.P7K8)

POETRY HANDBOOK, 4th ed., 1974, Funk & Wagnalls. (PN44.5.D4)

READER'S ADVISER AND BOOKMAN'S MANUAL, 2 vols., 11th ed., 1968–1969 Bowker. Selective bibliography with notes. (Z1035.B7)

READERS' GUIDE TO PERIODICAL LITERATURE, 1905–, Wilson. Look under Poems. (AI3.R496)

SUBJECT INDEX TO POETRY, 1940, American Library Association. A guide for adult readers. (PN1021.B7)

■B192   PROVERBS

MACMILLAN BOOK OF PROVERBS, MAXIMS, AND FAMILIAR PHRASES, by B. Stevenson, 1965, Macmillan. (PN6405.S8)

RACIAL PROVERBS; A SELECTION OF THE WORLD'S PROVERBS ARRANGED LINGUISTICALLY, by S. G. Champion, 2nd ed., 1950, Macmillan. (PN6405.C37)

PSEUDONYMS
See: B170.

PUBLISHING
See: B43.

QUOTATIONS
See: B44.

■B193   SHAKESPEARE

A CLASSIFIED SHAKESPEARE BIBLIOGRAPHY, 1936–1958, 1963, Pennsylvania State University. Covers standard bibliographies. Very useful. (Z8811.S64)

THE CONCISE ENCYCLOPEDIC GUIDE TO SHAKESPEARE, 1971, Horizon. Alphabetically arranged. (PR2892.M39)

HOME BOOK OF SHAKESPEARE QUOTATIONS, 1966, Scribner's. Topical arrangement with a glossary of unusual and archaic words. (PR2892.S63)

THE MAJOR SHAKESPEAREAN TRAGEDIES: A CRITICAL BIBLIOGRAPHY, 1973, Free. Full annotations, both descriptive and evaluative. (Z8812.Q54)

NEW AND COMPLETE CONCORDANCE OR VERBAL INDEX TO WORDS, PHRASES, AND PASSAGES IN THE DRAMATIC WORKS OF SHAKESPEARE, by J. Bartlett, 1894, Macmillan. Most complete index to Shakespeare's works. (PR2892.B34)

THE READER'S ENCYCLOPEDIA OF SHAKESPEARE, 1966, Crowell. Dictionary arrangement with a concise and very readable style. (PR2892.C3)

A SHAKESPEARE COMPANION, by F. E. Halliday, 1952. Funk. Complete coverage including summaries of his plays, data on editions, and so forth. Bibliographies. (PR2892.H3)

SHAKESPEARE-LEXICON: A COMPLETE DICTIONARY OF ALL THE ENGLISH WORDS, PHRASES AND CONSTRUCTIONS IN THE WORKS OF THE POET, 6th ed., rev. and enl., 2 vols., 1971, Walter de Gruyter. (PR2892.S4)

WHO'S WHO IN SHAKESPEARE, by Robin May, 1973, Taplinger. (PR2892.M397)

WHO'S WHO IN SHAKESPEARE, by Peter Quennell, 1973, Morrow. Includes an extensive series of pictures. (PR2989.Q4)

WILLIAM SHAKESPEARE: A READER'S GUIDE, 1971 (repr.), Octagon. (PR2976.H32)

■B194   SHORT STORIES

SHORT STORY INDEX, 1953, supplements 1956, 1960, 1965, and 1969, Wilson. Intended for those readers over ten years of age. (Z5917.S5C6)

SUBJECT AND TITLE INDEX TO SHORT STORIES FOR CHILDREN, 1955, American Library Association. Provides a graded guide to those appearing in collections. (Z1037.A4924)

TWENTIETH-CENTURY SHORT STORY EXPLICATION, INTERPRETATIONS, rev. ed., 1968 and suppls. 1970, 1973, Shoe String Press. (Z5917.S5W33)

See also: B171

■B195   SPANISH LITERATURE

DICTIONARY OF SPANISH LITERATURE, by M. Newmork, 1956, Littlefield. A good starting point. (PQ6006.N4)

THEATER
See: B138, B180.

WRITING MARKETS
See: B43.

B196–B220   RELIGION,   PHILOSOPHY,   AND MYTHOLOGY
_____

■B196   ADDRESSES

YEARBOOK OF AMERICAN CHURCHES, 1932– (annual), National Council of the Churches of Christ in the United States of America. Data on all denominations in the United States and Canada. Includes colleges, seminaries, church-related organizations, and so forth. (BR513.Y4)

See also: B21.

■B197   ARCHAEOLOGY

ARCHAEOLOGICAL ENCYCLOPEDIA OF THE HOLY LAND, 1972, Putnam's. Concise and detailed. Scholarly. (DS111.A2N38)

BIBLICAL ARCHAEOLOGY, by G. E. Wright, rev. ed., 1963, Westminster. (BS621.W72)

See also: B223a

■B198   ATLASES

ATLAS OF THE BIBLE, 1957, Nelson. (BS620.G752)

ATLAS OF THE EARLY CHRISTIAN WORLD, 1959, Nelson. (G1030.M42)

BAKER'S BIBLE ATLAS, 1962, Baker Book. (BS630.P45)

HISTORICAL ATLAS OF RELGION IN AMERICA, 1962, Harper. Covers 1650-1960. (G1021.E4G3)

THE OXFORD BIBLE ATLAS, 1962, Oxford. (BS630.M35)

RAND McNALLY BIBLE ATLAS, 1956, Rand McNally. (BS630.K7)

WESTMINSTER HISTORICAL ATLAS OF THE BIBLE, rev. ed., 1956, Westminster. (BS630.W7)

■B199 BIBLE COMMENTARIES

ABINGDON BIBLE COMMENTARY, 1929, Abingdon. From a fairly liberal Protestant point of view. (BS491.E5)

A CATHOLIC COMMENTARY ON THE HOLY SCRIPTURE, 1953, Nelson. Based on Douay version. (BS491.07)

EXPOSITOR'S BIBLE, 6 vols., 1943, Eerdmans. (BS491.E92)

THE INTERPRETER'S BIBLE, 12 vols., 1951—1957, Abingdon. Comprehensive, scholarly, and liberal in point of view. (BS491.2.I55)

THE JEROME BIBLICAL COMMENTARY, 1968, Prentice-Hall. A successor to A CATHOLIC COMMENTARY ON HOLY SCRIPTURE. (BS491.2.B7)

WORD PICTURES IN THE NEW TESTAMENT, 6 vols., 1943, Broadman. Authoritative and scholarly, this is a cross between a Greek lexicon and commentary. (BS2341.R6)

THE WYCLIFFE BIBLE COMMENTARY, 1962, Moody. Conservative in tone. (BS491.2.P4)

See also: B207, B220.

■B200 BIBLE CONCORDANCES

ANALYTICAL CONCORDANCE TO THE BIBLE, rev. ed., 1955, Funk. (BS425.Y7)

A COMPLETE CONCORDANCE TO THE HOLY SCRIPTURES OF THE OLD AND NEW TESTAMENTS, by A. Cruden (various titles and publishers). (BS425.C8)

EXHAUSTIVE CONCORDANCE OF THE BIBLE, 1890, Abingdon. Lists every word in the King James version. (BS425.S8)

GREEK-ENGLISH ANALYTICAL CONCORDANCE OF THE GREEK-ENGLISH NEW TESTAMENT, 1963, Zondervan. (BS2302.S7)

HARPER'S TOPICAL CONCORDANCE, rev. ed., 1969, Zondervan. (BS432.J63)

NELSON'S COMPLETE CONCORDANCE OF THE REVISED
STANDARD VERSION OF THE BIBLE, 1957, Nelson.
(BS425.E4)
THE NEW WORLD IDEA INDEX TO THE HOLY BIBLE, 1972,
World. (BS432.N43)

■B201   BIBLE QUOTATIONS

THE HOME BOOK OF BIBLE QUOTATIONS, 1949, Harper.
Collection of well-known phrases and sayings from the King
James version of the Bible. (BS432.S667)
See also: B44.

BIBLE VERSES, LOCATION OF
See: B200

■B202   BIBLE VERSIONS AND TRANSLATIONS

AMERICAN REVISED VERSION, 1901, Nelson.
(BS190.A1.1901.N42)
AMPLIFIED BIBLE, 1965, Zondervan, (BS195.S6)
THE APOCRYPHA: ACCORDING TO THE AUTHORIZED
VERSION, 1953, Harper. (BS1692.)
THE APOCRYPHA, Revised Standard Version, 1957, Nelson.
(BS1692.)
THE BERKELEY VERSION OF THE HOLY BIBLE, translated
by Verkuyl, 1959, Zondervan. (BS195.B38)
CENTENARY TRANSLATION OF THE NEW
TESTAMENT . . . , translated by H.B. Montgomery, 1924,
Judson Press. (BS2095.M75)
THE COMPLETE BIBLE, AN AMERICAN TRANSLATION,
translated by J.M.P. Smith, and E.J. Goodspeed, 1939,
University of Chicago. (BS195.K5)
DOUAY VERSION, 1582–1610, Benziger Brothers.
(BS180.1852.N4)
THE HOLY BIBLE, translation by R.A. Knox, 1956, Sheed and
Ward (Roman Catholic). (BS195.K5)
THE HOLY SCRIPTURES ACCORDING TO THE MASORETIC
TEXT, 1955, Jewish Publication Society of America. (BS715.)
THE JERUSALEM BIBLE, 1966, Doubleday. (BS195.J4)
KING JAMES VERSION, 1611, various publications.
(BS185.1948.N4)

NEW ENGLISH BIBLE, 1970, published jointly by Cambridge and Oxford. (BS192.A11971.N42)

THE NEW TESTAMENT: A TRANSLATION IN PLAIN ENGLISH, translated by C.B. Williams, 1937, Moody. (BS2095.W515)

THE NEW TESTAMENT IN MODERN ENGLISH, translated by J.B. Phillips, 1958, Macmillan. (BS2095.P5)

THE NEW TESTAMENT IN MODERN SPEECH, translated by R.F. Weymouth, 1943, Pilgrim Press. (RS2095.W45)

THE NEW TESTAMENT OCTAPLA, 1962, Nelson. Eight English translations, side by side. (BS2024.1962.W4)

A NEW TRANSLATION OF THE BIBLE, translated by J. Moffatt, 1925, Harper. (BS195.M615)

REVISED STANDARD VERSION, 1946–1952, Nelson. (BS191.A11952.N4)

■B203   BIBLES, BIBLIOGRAPHY

THE ENGLISH BIBLE: A HISTORY OF TRANSLATIONS FROM THE EARLIEST ENGLISH VERSIONS TO THE NEW ENGLISH BIBLE, 1970, Oxford. (BS455.B74)

THE ENGLISH BIBLE IN AMERICA. . . EDITIONS OF . . . 1777–1957, 1961, American Bible Society and the New York Public Library. (Z771.A5H5)

THE READER'S ADVISER AND BOOKMAN'S MANUAL, 2 vols., 11th ed., 1968–1969, (revised frequently), Bowker. (Z1035.B7)

■B204   BIBLIOGRAPHY, GENERAL

A BIBLIOGRAPHICAL GUIDE TO THE HISTORY OF CHRISTIANITY, by S.J. Case, 1951, Peter Smith. Selected representative titles. Some evaluative notes. (Z7777.C33)

A BIBLIOGRAPHY OF BIBLIOGRAPHIES IN RELIGION, by J.G. Barrow, 1955, Edwards. Arranged by subject field. (Z7751.B33)

A CRITICAL BIBLIOGRAPHY OF RELIGION IN AMERICA, by N.R. Burr, 2 vols., 1961, Princeton University. Reviews the literature of the subject in a running organized comment. (BR515.S6)

CRITICAL GUIDE TO CATHOLIC REFERENCE BOOKS, 1971, Libraries Unlimited. (Z674.R4)

DOCTORAL DISSERTATIONS IN THE FIELD OF RELIGION,
1940–1952, 1954, Columbia. (Z7751.C7)
ENCOUNTER WITH BOOK: A GUIDE TO CHRISTIAN
READING, 1970, Inter-Varsity. Annotated. (Z7751.E53)
INTERNATIONAL DIRECTORY OF RELIGIOUS
INFORMATION SYSTEMS, 1971, Marquette. Covers 66
agencies in the U.S. and abroad. (BL35.M62)
PHILOSOPHIC ABSTRACTS, 1939–1954, Moore. (B1.P46)
RELIGION IN AMERICAN LIFE, 1971, Appleton. (Z7757.U5B8)
RELIGIONS, MYTHOLOGIES, FOLKLORES: AN
ANNOTATED BIBLIOGRAPHY, by K.S. Diehl, 2nd ed.,
1962, Scarecrow. A classified list covering faith and practice in
all cultures. (Z7751.D54)
See also: B11.

■ **B205 BIOGRAPHY**

DICTIONARY OF CHRISTIAN BIOGRAPHY, LITERATURE,
SECTS, AND DOCTRINES, by W. Smith, 4 vols., 1877–
1887. (BR95.S65)
WHO WAS WHO IN CHURCH HISTORY, 1963, Moody. Sketches
of 1750 men and women from the time of Christ to the present.
(BR1700.M64)
WHO'S WHO IN THE NEW TESTAMENT, 1972, Holt. Well il-
lustrated. Arranged alphabetically. (BS2430.B67)
WHO'S WHO IN THE OLD TESTAMENT, 1972, Holt. Well il-
lustrated. Arranged alphabetically. (BS570.C64)
See also: A5–A6, B11a, B207, B210, B213.

CHURCH HISTORY
See: B213.

■ **B205a COMPARATIVE RELIGION**

DICTIONARY OF COMPARATIVE RELIGION, 1970, Scribner's.
Compact, covering both living and dead religions. (BL31.D54)
RELIGIONS OF THE WORLD FROM PRIMITIVE BELIEFS TO
MODERN FAITHS, 1971, Grosset & Dunlap. Excellent
Index. (BL80.2.P346)
See also: A1, B213.

■ **B206 DENOMINATIONAL DATA**

HANDBOOK OF DENOMINATIONS IN THE U.S., 5th ed.,
1970, Abingdon. Covers history and basic beliefs. Extensive
bibliography. (BR516.5.M38)

HISTORICAL ATLAS OF RELIGION IN AMERICA, 1962, Harper. General statistics from 1650–1960. (G1201.E4G3)

THE RELIGIOUS BODIES OF AMERICA, by F. Mayer, 4th ed., 1961, Concordia. Covers doctrines, practices, and history of each. (BR516.5.M3)

WHAT AMERICANS BELIEVE AND HOW THEY WORSHIP, rev. ed., 1962, Harper. (BR516.5.W5)

YEARBOOK OF AMERICAN CHURCHES, 1937– (annual), National Council of the Churches of Christ in the United States of America. Brief data on all denominations. The most comprehensive. (BR513.Y4)

See also: B213.

■B207 DICTIONARIES

THE CATHOLIC DICTIONARY, 1958, Macmillan. (BX841.C35)

A DICTIONARY OF LIFE IN BIBLE TIMES, 1960, Oxford. Brief, with good illustrations. (BS621.C653)

THE DICTIONARY OF PHILOSOPHY, by D.D. Runes, 1952, Philosophical Library. (B41.R8)

DICTIONARY OF PHILOSOPHY AND PSYCHOLOGY, by J.M. Baldwin, 3 vols., 1925, Macmillan. Out of date, but still usable because of its very complete coverage. (B41.B3)

DICTIONARY OF THE BIBLE, by J. Hastings, 5 vols., 1898–1904, T. and T. Clark (also a new one-volume edition, 1962, Scribner's). Comprehensive and good on topics that are not dated. (BS44.H5)

DICTIONARY OF THE BIBLE, by J.L. McKenzie, 1967, Bruce. Catholic emphasis. (BS440.M36)

HARPER'S BIBLE DICTIONARY, 8th ed., 1973, Harper. Useful. (BS440.M52)

THE INTERPRETER'S DICTIONARY, 4 vols., 1962, Abingdon. Comprehensive, authoritative, and scholarly. (BS44.I63)

THE NEW BIBLE DICTIONARY, 1962, Eerdmans. Authoritative and scholarly. (BS440.D6)

NEW WESTMINSTER DICTIONARY OF THE BIBLE, rev. ed., 1970, Westminister. (BS440.G4)

UNGER'S BIBLE DICTIONARY, 1958, Moody. Good format and very useful. (BS440.U5)

See also: A7, B220.

DISSERTATIONS IN RELIGION
See: B204.

■B207a ETHICS

BAKER'S DICTIONARY OF CHRISTIAN ETHICS, 1973, Baker.
(BJ1199.B34)
DICTIONARY OF CHRISTIAN ETHICS, 1967, Westminister.
(BJ63.M3)
See also: B210, B213.

FOLKLORE
See: B208.

LEGEND
See: B208.

■B208 MYTHOLOGY

A BIBLIOGRAPHY OF NORTH AMERICAN FOLKLORE AND
FOLKSONGS, 1951, Greenberg. Comprehensive list of books,
articles, records, and such, with some explanatory notes.
(Z5984.U5H3)
BULFINCH'S MYTHOLOGY, rev. ed., 1970, Crowell. A standard
work dealing with classical mythology. (BL310.B82)
CROWELL'S HANDBOOK OF CLASSICAL MYTHOLOGY,
1970, Crowell. Alphabetically arranged. (BL303.T75)
A DICTIONARY OF BRITISH FOLK-TALES IN THE ENGLISH
LANGUAGE, 2 vols., 1970–1971, Indiana. Covers folk
narratives and legends. Other volumes to follow. (GR141.B68)
DICTIONARY OF MYTHOLOGY, FOLKLORE, AND
SYMBOLS, by G. Jobes, 3 vols., 1961–1963, Scarecrow.
Covers all cultures, religions, and civilizations from the begin-
ning of recorded history to the present. (GR35.J6)
ENCYCLOPAEDIA OF RELIGION AND ETHICS, by J.
Hastings, 13 vols., 1908–1927, Scribner's. Covers
mythological aspects of living and ancient
religions.(BL31.E44)
FUNK AND WAGNALLS STANDARD DICTIONARY OF
FOLKLORE, MYTHOLOGY AND LEGEND, 2 vols., 1949–
1950, Funk. Authoritive with selected bibliographies.
(GR35.F8)
MYTHOLOGY OF ALL RACES, 13 vols., 1916–1932, Cooper.
Includes illustrations and excellent index. (BL25.M8)

See also: A1, B207, B213.

■B209 PERIODICAL INDEXES

CATHOLIC PERIODICAL INDEX, 1939–, Catholic Library Association. Coverage begins with 1930. (AI3.C3)

CHRISTIAN PERIODICAL INDEX, 1956–1960, 1961– (quarterly), Buffalo Bible Institute Bookstore. (Z7753.C5)

ESSAY AND GENERAL LITERATURE INDEX, 1900–, Wilson. Useful. (AI3.E752)

INDEX TO RELIGIOUS PERIODICAL LITERATURE, 1949–, American Library Association. Covers over sixty periodicals and includes book reviews. (Z7753.A5)

NEW TESTAMENT ABSTRACTS, 1956– (three times a year), Weston College. Covers Catholic, Jewish, and Protestant periodicals in many languages. (BS410.N35)

THE NEW YORK TIMES INDEX, 1851–, The New York Times. Good for current information and complete text of documents. (AI21.N44)

READER'S GUIDE TO PERIODICAL LITERATURE, 1900–, Wilson. General information. (AI3.R496)

RELIGIOUS AND THEOLOGICAL ABSTRACTS, 1958– (quarterly), Theological Publications, Inc. A selected list of religious periodicals, including Christian, Jewish, and Moslem journals. (BR1.R286)

SOCIAL SCIENCES AND HUMANITIES INDEX, 1907–, Wilson. Very useful for both religion and philosophy. (AI3.R49) Since 1974—these are two separate indexes.

■B210 PHILOSOPHY

ABSTRACTS See: B204.

GENERAL WORKS

THE CONCISE ENCYCLOPEDIA OF WESTERN PHILOSOPHY, 1960, Hawthorn. Brief articles on persons and ideas of all times. (B41.U7)

DICTIONARY OF THE HISTORY OF IDEAS, 4 vols., 1973 and Index vol., 1974, Scribner's. Interdisciplinary in scope. (CB5.D52)

ENCYCLOPAEDIA OF RELIGION AND ETHICS, by J. Hastings, 13 vols., 1908–1927, Scribner's. Good for general information. (BL31.E44)

THE ENCYCLOPEDIA OF PHILOSOPHY, 8 vols., 1967, Collier-Macmillan. Comprehensive with annotated bibliographies. (B41.E5)

MASTERPIECES OF WORLD PHILOSOPHY IN SUMMARY FORM, 2 vols., 1961, Salem. (B21.M3)

See also: B207, B209, B213

■B211   POPES

POPES THROUGH THE AGES, rev. ed., 1964, Van Nostrand. (BX955.B77)

See also: B213.

PRIMITIVE RELIGION

See: A1, B213, B258.

■B212   PRONUNCIATION GUIDE

THE VOCABULARY OF THE CHURCH, A PRONUNCIATION GUIDE, 1960, Macmillan. (BR95.W53)

See also: A7, B207.

■B213   RELIGIONS

GENERAL WORKS

CONCISE DICTIONARY OF THE CHRISTIAN WORLD MISSION, 1971, Abingdon. Concise, comprehensive, very useful. (BV2040.N44)

A DICTIONARY OF NON-CHRISTIAN RELIGIONS, 1973, Westminister. (B131.P36)

DOCUMENTS OF THE CHRISTIAN CHURCH, 2nd ed., 1963, Oxford. A valuable collection of important early church documents. (BR141.B4)

ENCYCLOPAEDIA OF RELIGION AND ETHICS, by J. Hastings, 13 vols., 1908–1927, Scribner's. An outstanding general reference guide. (BL31.E44)

ENCYCLOPEDIA OF BUDDHISM, 3 vols., 1973, International Publications Service. (See Card Catalog)

ENCYCLOPEDIA OF ISLAM, 5 vols., new ed., 1954–1974, Humanities. (Leiden, Brill). One of the most important works in English on Islamic subjects. (DS37.E523)

THE HINDU WORLD: AN ENCYCLOPEDIC SURVEY OF HINDUISM, 2 vols., 1968, Praeger. (BL1105.W34)

THE JEWISH ENCYCLOPEDIA, 12 vols., 1901−1906, Funk. Treats many other religions besides Judaism. (DS102.8.J65)

NEW CATHOLIC ENCYCLOPEDIA, 15 vols., 1967, McGraw-Hill. Comprehensive. (BX841.N44)

NEW SCHAFF-HERZOG ENCYCLOPEDIA OF RELIGIOUS KNOWLEDGE, 13 vols., 1951, Baker. Comprehensive and authoritative. (BR95.S435)

OXFORD DICTIONARY OF THE CHRISTIAN CHURCH, 2nd ed., 1974, Oxford. (BR95.08)

See also: A1.

HISTORY

AMERICAN CHRISTIANITY, by H.S. Smith, 2 vols., 1962−1963, Scribner's. Covers 1607 to 1960. (BS514.S55)

CHRISTIANITY IN A REVOLUTIONARY AGE, 5 vols., 1958−1962, Harper. Subtitle: A History of Christianity in the Nineteenth and Twentieth Centuries. (BR477.L3)

HISTORICAL ATLAS OF RELIGION IN AMERICA, 1962, Harper. Brief. (G1201.E4G3)

HISTORY OF THE CHRISTIAN CHURCH, 8 vols., 1889−1910, Eerdmans. Covers from A.D. 1 to the Swiss Reformation. (BR145.S3)

A HISTORY OF THE EXPANSION OF CHRISTIANITY, 7 vols., 1937−1945, Harper. Traces the development of Christianity from its beginnings through World War II. Bibliographies. (BR145.L3)

A SOURCE BOOK FOR ANCIENT CHURCH HISTORY, 1970, AMS. Follows a chronological analysis and grouping of topics. (BR160.A2A9)

See also: General works above.

■B214 RELIGIOUS EDUCATION

EDUCATION INDEX, 1929−, Wilson. Very useful. (Z5813.E23)

RESEARCHES IN PERSONALITY, CHARACTER AND RELIGIOUS EDUCATION: A BIBLIOGRAPHY OF AMERICAN DOCTORAL DISSERTATIONS, 1885−1959, 1962, University of Pittsburgh. (Z7849.L54)

THE WESTMINSTER DICTIONARY OF CHRISTIAN EDUCATION, 1963, Westminster. Comprehensively covers ideas, personalities, methods, and practical questions in contemporary Christian education. (BV1461.C8)

■B215 RELIGIOUS HOLIDAYS

AMERICAN BOOK OF DAYS, 1948, Wilson. (GI4803.D6)
See also: A3, B19.

■B216 RELIGIOUS PUBLICATIONS

AYER'S DIRECTORY OF NEWSPAPERS AND PERIODICALS, 1880– (annual), Ayer. (Z6951.Z97)
ULRICH'S INTERNATIONAL DIRECTORY, 15th ed., (biennial), Bowker. (Z6941.U5)

■B217 RELIGIOUS SCHOOLS

YEARBOOK OF AMERICAN CHURCHES (annual), National Council of the Churches of Christ in the United States of America. (BR513.Y4)

■B218 RELIGIOUS SECTS

DICTIONARY OF AMERICAN HISTORY, 6 vols., 1942, supplement 1961, Scribner's. (E174.A43)
See also: A1, B206, B213.

■B219 STATISTICS

HISTORICAL ATLAS OF RELIGION IN AMERICA, 1962, Harper. Covers 1650–1960. (G1201.E4G3)
YEARBOOK OF AMERICAN CHURCHES (annual). National Council of the Churches of Christ in the United States of America. Covers different types of statistical and historical information on all denominations. (BR513.Y4)
See also: A2–A3, also individual denominational annuals.

■B220 THEOLOGY

BAKER'S DICTIONARY OF THEOLOGY, 1961, Baker. (BR95.B25)
A COMPANION TO THE BIBLE, 1958, Oxford. Covers major theological terms and ideas found in the Bible. (BS440.A473)
A DICTIONARY OF CHRISTIAN THEOLOGY, 1969, Westminster. (BR95.R47)
THEOLOGICAL DICTIONARY OF THE NEW TESTAMENT, edited by G. Kittel, 7 vols., 1964– (English translation), Eerdmans. Scholarly and indispensable for the interpretation of the New Testament. (PA881.K513)

THEOLOGICAL DICTIONARY OF THE OLD TESTAMENT, 12 vols., 1974–, Eerdmans. Alphabetical. Treats words theologically and philologically. Draws from an international team of scholars. (BS440.B5713)

A THEOLOGICAL WORD BOOK OF THE BIBLE, 1950, Macmillan. Covers words of prime importance. (BS440.R53)

See also: B207, B209, B213.

B221–B252 SCIENCE

■B221 AERONAUTICS

AEROSPACE YEAR BOOK, 1919– (annual), American Aviation Publications. Gives the year's developments in the industry, general information, and statistics. (TL501.A563)

HANDBOOK OF ASTRONAUTICAL ENGINEERING, 1963, McGraw-Hill. Provides a comprehensive summary of technical and engineering data. (TL794.K6)

See also: B236, B238, B248.

■B222 AGRICULTURE

AMERICAN MEN AND WOMEN OF SCIENCE, AGRICULTURAL, ANIMAL AND VETERINARY SCIENCES, 1974, Bowker. (Q141.A47)

A DICTIONARY OF AGRICULTURE AND ALLIED TERMINOLOGY, 1962, University of Michigan. (S411.D57)

LITERATURE OF AGRICULTURAL RESEARCH, by J.R. Blanchard, 1958, University of California. Classified and annotated. (Z5071.B5)

YEARBOOK OF AGRICULTURE, 1895– (annual), U.S. Government Printing Office. Covers a different broad subject each year. (S21.A35)

See also: B248.

■B223 ANATOMY

ANATOMY OF THE HUMAN BODY, by H. Gray, 29th ed., 1973, Lea and Febiger. The classic in its field. (QM23.G7)

ATLAS OF HUMAN ANATOMY, 3 vols., 9th ed., 1974, Hafner. Very well illustrated. (QM25.S675)

See also: B238.

■B223a ARCHAEOLOGY

BEGINNER'S GUIDE TO ARCHAEOLOGY, 1973, Stackpole. (E77.9.B73)
THE CONCISE ENCYCLOPEDIA OF ARCHAEOLOGY, 2nd ed., 1971, Hawthorn. (CC70.C6)
LAROUSSE ENCYCLOPEDIA OF ARCHAEOLOGY, 1972, Putnam's. World wide in scope. (CC165.C4313)
See also: B162, B197.

■B224 ASTRONOMY

THE AMERICAN EPHEMERIS AND NAUTICAL ALMANAC, 1852– (annual), U.S. Government Printing Office. Lists all astronomical and meteorological data needed by the marine navigator. (QB8.U1)
ANNUAL REVIEW OF ASTRONOMY AND ASTROPHYSICS, (annual), Annual Reviews. Covers latest developments. (QB1.A2884)
THE NEW GUIDE TO THE PLANETS, 1971, Norton. Brief but good. (QB501.M688)
See also: B238.

■B225 ATOMIC ENERGY

ATOMIC ENERGY DESKBOOK, by J.F. Hogerton, 1963, Reinhold. Primarily concerned with the peaceful uses of atomic power; gives essential facts. (QC772.H64)
See also: B238, B249.

■B226 BIBLIOGRAPHY, GENERAL

THE AAAS SCIENCE BOOK LIST. A SELECTED AND ANNOTATED LIST OF SCIENCE AND MATHEMATICS BOOKS FOR SECONDARY SCHOOL STUDENTS, COLLEGE UNDERGRADUATES, AND NONSPECIALISTS, 3rd ed., 1970, AAAS. (Q181.A1A68)
SCIENCE FOR SOCIETY: A BIBLIOGRAPHY, 3rd ed., 1972, AAAS. Concerned with social problems. Short annotations. (Z7405.S6)
SCIENCE REFERENCE SOURCES, 5th ed., 1969, M.I.T. A selective list arranged by broad subject field. (Z7401.J4)
SCIENTIFIC, TECHNICAL AND ENGINEERING SOCIETY PUBLICATIONS IN PRINT, 1972–, Bowker. (Z7911.K92)
See also: B11.

■ B227 BIOGRAPHY

AMERICAN MEN AND WOMEN OF SCIENCE, 12th ed., 7 vols., 1971–1973, Bowker. Gives key facts on scientists and researchers active in the physical and biological sciences. (Q141.A47)

DICTIONARY OF SCIENTIFIC BIOGRAPHY, 12 vols., 1970–, Scribner's. Covers all region and historical periods giving concise information on individuals and account of his work in relation to his predecessors, contemporaries and successors. (Q141.D5)

GREAT CHEMISTS, 1961, Wiley. (QD21.F35)

INDEX TO SCIENTISTS OF THE WORLD, FROM ANCIENT TO MODERN TIMES, 1962, Faxon. Covers biographies, portraits, and chief scientific contributions. (Z7404.I7)

WHO'S WHO IN SOVIET SCIENCE AND TECHNOLOGY, 1960, Telberg. Current information. (Q127.R9W5)

WHO'S WHO OF BRITISH SCIENTISTS, 1971, Ohio. (Q145.D52)

See also: A5–A6.

■ B228 BIOLOGY

BIOLOGY DATA BOOK, 2nd ed., 3 vols., 1972–1974, FASEB. (QH310.A392)

BIOLOGIST'S HANDBOOK OF PRONUNCIATIONS, 1960, C.C. Thomas. (QH13.J3)

A DICTIONARY OF BIOLOGICAL TERMS, by I.F. Henderson, 8th ed., 1963, Van Nostrand. (QH13.H38)

A DICTIONARY OF BIOLOGY, 6th ed., 1973, Penguin. (QH13.A25)

THE ENCYCLOPEDIA OF THE BIOLOGICAL SCIENCES, edited by P. Gray, 2nd ed., 1970, Van Nostrand Reinhold. Comprehensive and authoritative. (QH13.G7)

STUDENT DICTIONARY OF BIOLOGY, 1973, Van Nostrand Reinhold. (QH13.A25)

HANDBOOK OF BIOLOGICAL DATA, by W. Spector, 1956, Saunders. Basic data in condensed tabular form. (QH310.S6)

SOURCE BOOK OF BIOLOGICAL NAMES AND TERMS, 3rd ed., 1972, C.C. Thomas. Gives origins and meanings, including many examples of use. (QH83.J3)

See also: B238, B248.

■B229 BOTANY

COLLEGIATE DICTIONARY OF BOTANY, 1971, Ronald. (QK9.S88)

A DICTIONARY OF THE FLOWERING PLANTS AND FERNS, 8th ed., 1973, Cambridge. Comprehensive and scholarly. (QK11.W53)

GLOSSARY OF BOTANIC TERMS, 4th ed., 1953, Hafner. (QK9.J3)

GRAY'S MANUAL OF BOTANY, 8th ed., 1950, American Book. Standard in its field. (QK117.G75)

HORTUS SECOND, by L.H. Bailey, 1941, Macmillan. A standard authoritative work covering North America. (SB45.B22)

KNOW YOUR WOODS: A COMPLETE GUIDE TO TREES, WOODS, AND VENEERS, 1972, Scibner's. Comprehensive with detailed index. (SD434.C65)

STANDARD CYCLOPEDIA OF HORTICULTURE, 3 vols., 1947, Macmillan. Very comprehensive, including biographies, bibliographies, and full indexes. (SB45.B17)

See also: B248

■B230 CANCER

ADVANCES IN CANCER RESEARCH, 1953– (annual), Academic. Covers various topics. (RC267.A45)

See also: B238, B248.

■B231 CHEMISTRY

AGRICULTURAL

YEARBOOK OF AGRICULTURE (annual). U.S. Government Printing Office. Covers a different broad subject each year. (S21.A35)

BIBLIOGRAPHY

CHEMICAL PUBLICATIONS, 4th ed., 1965, McGraw-Hill. Designed as an introduction to the sources of chemical literature. (Z5521.M52)

A GUIDE TO THE LITERATURE OF CHEMISTRY, 2nd ed., 1957, Wiley. Very useful and complete. (Z5521.C89)

HOW TO FIND OUT IN CHEMISTRY, 1965, Pergamon. (Z5521.B9)

DICTIONARIES

THE CONDENSED CHEMICAL DICTIONARY, by A. Rose and

E.G. Rose, 8th ed., 1971, Reinhold. Useful for products and trade names. (QD5.C5)

DICTIONARY OF NAMED EFFECTS AND LAWS IN CHEMISTRY, 2nd rev. ed., 1961, Macmillan. (Q123.B3)

GLOSSARY OF ORGANIC CHEMISTRY, by S. Patai, 1962, Wiley. (QD251.P25)

HACKH'S CHEMICAL DICTIONARY, 4th ed., 1969, McGraw-Hill. (QD5.H3)

GENERAL WORKS

ANNUAL REPORTS ON THE PROGRESS OF CHEMISTRY, 1904− (annual), Chemical Society, London. Covers advancements of chemistry as a whole. (QD1.C57)

ENCYCLOPEDIA OF CHEMISTRY, 3rd ed., 1973, Van Nostrand Reinhold. Covers all phases of chemistry and allied sciences. (QD5.E58)

HISTORY

HISTORY OF CHEMISTRY, by J. Partington, 4 vols., 1962−1967, St. Martin's. (QD11.P28)

INDUSTRIAL

ADVANCES IN CHEMICAL ENGINEERING, 1956− (annual), Academic. (TP145.A4)

CHEMICAL ENGINEERING THESAURUS, 1961, American Institute of Chemical Engineers. (Z699.5.C5A6)

CHEMICAL ENGINEERS HANDBOOK, 5th ed., 1974, McGraw-Hill. Covers most every type of reference date needed by the chemical engineer. (TD155.C42)

ENCYCLOPEDIA OF CHEMICAL TECHNOLOGY, 18 vols., 2nd ed., 1963−1972, Wiley. An indispensable work giving a comprehensive summary of industrial knowledge on materials, processes, and equipment. (TP9.E685)

THORPE'S DICTIONARY OF APPLIED CHEMISTRY, 4th ed., 12 vols., 1937−1956, Longmans. A standard guide to industrial chemistry. (TP9.T72)

INORGANIC

COMPREHENSIVE INORGANIC CHEMISTRY, 5 vols., 1973, Pergamon.

ENCYCLOPEDIA OF CHEMICAL REACTIONS, 8 vols., 1946−1959, Reinhold. An attempt to list all known inorganic chemical reactions published in all literature on the subject. (QD155.J3)

MELLOR'S COMPREHENSIVE TREATISE ON INORGANIC AND THEORETICAL CHEMISTRY, 16 vols., 1922–1937, supplements 1956 and 1961, Longmans. Comprehensive with good bibliographies. Gives complete description of all elements and compounds known in inorganic chemistry. (QD31.M52)

ORGANIC

BEILSTEIN'S HANDBUCH DER ORGANISCHEN CHEMIE, 4th ed., 1918–, J. Springer, Berlin. A monumental compilation providing a complete summary of published data on organic compounds known to date. It reigns supreme as the general reference work in the field. (QD251.B4)

CHEMISTRY OF CARBON COMPOUNDS, 5 vols., 2nd rev. ed., 1964–, Elsevier. A comprehensive treatise. (QD251.R62)

DICTIONARY OF ORGANIC COMPOUNDS, 5 vols. and supplement 1965, Oxford. Gives the constitution and the physical and chemical properties of the principal carbon compounds and their derivatives. (QD251.D49)

ORGANIC ANALYSIS (annual), 1953–, Interscience. (QD271.07)

THE RING INDEX, 1960 and supplements, American Chemical Society. (QD291.P)

TABLES

HANDBOOK OF CHEMICAL DATA, 1957, Reinhold. (QD65.H27)

HANDBOOK OF CHEMISTRY AND PHYSICS, 1914– (annual), Chemical Rubber. (QD65.H3)

LANGE'S HANDBOOK OF CHEMISTRY, 11th ed., 1973, (revised frequently), McGraw-Hill. Arrangement largely in tabular form. (TP151.H25)

TABLES OF PHYSICAL AND CHEMICAL CONSTANTS, 14th ed., 1973, Wiley. (QC61.K3)

TRADE NAMES

CHEMICAL SYNONYMS AND TRADE NAMES, 7th ed., 1971, CRC. (TP9.G28)

CHEMICAL TRADE NAMES AND COMMERCIAL SYNONYMS, 2nd ed., 1955, Van Nostrand. Lists names

applied to various chemical substances and gives brief information on each. (TP9.H3)
See also: B238.

■B232   DICTIONARIES, GENERAL WORKS

CHAMBERS DICTIONARY OF SCIENCE AND TECHNOLOGY, 1972, Barnes & Noble. Comprehensive and authorative. (T9.C5)

DICTIONARY OF BUSINESS AND SCIENTIFIC TERMS, 1961, Gulf. (Q123.T85)

DICTIONARY OF TECHNICAL TERMS, 11th ed., 1970, Bruce. Terms used in trades, mass production, shopwork, and technical procedures. (T9.C885)

McGRAW-HILL DICTIONARY OF SCIENTIFIC AND TECHNICAL TERMS, 1974, McGraw-Hill. (See Card Catalog)

See also: Under specific field, Chemistry, and so forth.

■B233   DRUGS

THE BIOLOGY OF ALCOHOLISM, 4 vols., 1970–, Plenum. (RC565.K52)

ENCYCLOPEDIA OF CHEMICAL TECHNOLOGY, 18 vols., 2nd ed., 1963–, 1972, Wiley. An indispensable work giving a comprehensive summary of industrial knowledge on materials, processes, and equipment. (TP9.E685)

THE MERCK INDEX, 8th ed., 1968, Merck. Each listing gives chemical names, popular names, methods of preparation, and so forth. (RS356.M524)

THE NATIONAL DIRECTORY OF DRUG ABUSE TREATMENT PROGRAMS, 1972, Super. of Documents. (See Card Catalog)

YEARBOOK OF DRUG ABUSE, 1973– (annual), Behavioral. Survey articles, descriptions of the drug scene and treatment programs, and bibliographies accompany each article. (HV5825.Y4)

THE UNITED STATES DISPENSATORY, 27th ed., 1973, Lippincott. A collection of articles, alphabetically arranged, about individual drugs and their proper use. (RS151.2.D5)

■B234   ECOLOGY

ANNUAL REVIEW OF ECOLOGY AND SYSTEMATICS, (annual), Annual Reviews. (QH540.A53)

THE COMPLETE ECOLOGY FACT BOOK, 1972, Doubleday. (TP174.N6)

DICTIONARY OF ECOLOGY, by H. C. Hansen, 1962, Philosophical Library. Covers new terms and many words from related fields. (QH541.H25)

See also: B228, B238, B248.

∎B235 ELECTRONICS

BIBLIOGRAPHY OF THE HISTORY OF ELECTRONICS, 1972, Scarecrow. (Z5836.S54)

BUCHSBAUM'S COMPLETE HANDBOOK OF PRACTICAL ELECTRONIC REFERENCE DATA, 1973, Prentice-Hall. Emphasis is on practical aspects. (TK7825.B8)

DICTIONARY OF ELECTRONICS ABBREVIATIONS, SIGNS, AND SYMBOLS, 1965, Odyssey. (TK7804.D48)

HANDBOOK OF MODERN ELECTRONIC DATA, 1973, Reston. Arranged in topical groupings. (TK7825.M27)

IEEE STANDARD DICTIONARY OF ELECTRICAL AND ELECTRONICS TERMS, 1972, Wiley. Indispensable. (TK9.I478)

THE INTERNATIONAL DICTIONARY OF PHYSICS AND ELECTRONICS, 2nd ed., 1961, Van Nostrand. Extensive treatment with good cross-references. (QC5.I5)

MODERN DICTIONARY OF ELECTRONICS, 4th ed., 1972, Bobbs-Merrill. Covers over 18,000 terms. (TK7804.M6)

See also: B238, B249.

∎B236 ENGINEERING

ELECTRICAL ENGINEER'S HANDBOOK, 2 vols., 1949–1950, Wiley. Covers electric power, electric communications, and electronics. (TK151.P42)

ENCYCLOPEDIA OF ENGINEERING MATERIALS, 1963, Reinhold. Covers all basic engineering materials. (TA403.E47)

ENGINEERING ENCYCLOPEDIA, 3rd ed., 1963, Industrial Press. Concise, covering all phases of engineering. (TA9.J65)

ENGINEERING INDEX THESAURUS, 1972, CCM Information Corp. (Z695.1.E5E48)

HANDBOOK OF ASTRONAUTICAL ENGINEERING, 1962, McGraw-Hill. Guide to modern space-flight technology. (TL794.K6)

INDUSTRIAL ENGINEERING HANDBOOK, rev. ed., 1963, McGraw-Hill. (T56.M38)

PLANT ENGINEERING HANDBOOK, 2nd ed., 1959, McGraw-Hill. Covers plant organization design, construction, operation, and maintenance, showing how industrial plants can be run more efficiently and economically. (TS155.S758)

SOURCES OF ENGINEERING INFORMATION, 1948, University of California. (Z5851.D3)

STANDARD HANDBOOK FOR MECHANICAL ENGINEERS, 7th ed., 1968, McGraw-Hill. Standard work in its field. (TJ151.S82)

THESAURUS OF ENGINEERING AND SCIENTIFIC TERMS, 1967, Engineers Joint Council. A vocabulary reference for indexing and retrieving of technical information. (Z6951.1.E5.E5)

See also: B231.

EVOLUTION
See: B228, B238, B258.

■**B237   FOOD**

THE CHEMISTRY AND TECHNOLOGY OF FOOD AND FOOD PRODUCTS, 3 vols., 2nd ed., 1951, Interscience. Scholarly and comprehensive. (TX531.J33)

ENCYCLOPEDIA OF CHEMICAL TECHNOLOGY, 18 vols., 2nd ed., 1963−1972, Wiley. An indispensable work; a comprehensive summary of industrial knowledge on materials, processes, and equipment. (TP9.E685)

INTERNATIONAL DICTIONARY OF FOOD AND COOKING, 1974, Hastings. (TX349.M33)

■**B238   GENERAL WORKS AND HISTORIES OF SCIENCE**

A GUIDE TO THE HISTORY OF SCIENCE, by G. Sarton, 1952, Chronica Botanica Co. Includes a classified bibliography of the subject. (Q125.S24)

A HISTORY OF TECHNOLOGY, 5 vols., 1954−1958, Oxford. Scholarly and readable account of the development of technology from earliest times, chronologically arranged. (T15.S53)

INTRODUCTION TO THE HISTORY OF SCIENCE, by G. Sarton, 3 vols., 1927−1948, Williams & Wilkins. From Homer to the fourteenth century, including good biographies and bibliographies. (Q125.S32)

McGRAW-HILL ENCYCLOPEDIA OF SCIENCE AND TECHNOLOGY, 15 vols., 3rd ed., 1971, and yearbooks, 1961–, McGraw-Hill. Very comprehensive. One should use the index volume. (Q121.M3)

SMITHSONIAN INSTITUTION, 1847– (annual). U.S. Government Printing Office. Very useful and authoritative. (Q11.S66)

VAN NOSTRAND'S SCIENTIFIC ENCYCLOPEDIA, 4th ed., 1968, Van Nostrand. (Q121.V3)

See also: A1.

■B239   GENETICS

ADVANCES IN GENETICS, 1947– (annual), Academic. Covers various topics. (QH431.A1A3)

A DICTIONARY OF GENETICS, 2nd ed., 1972, Oxford. Covers about 5,000 terms. (QH431.K518)

See also: B248.

■B240   GEOGRAPHY

AIDS TO GEOGRAPHICAL RESEARCH, 1971, (repr.), Greenwood. A selective bibliography including books, periodicals, and maps. (Z6001.A1W9)

A DICTIONARY OF GEOGRAPHY, by F. J. Monkhouse, 2nd ed., 1970, Aldine. (G103.M6)

DICTIONARY OF GEOGRAPHY, ed. by Sir Dudley Stamp, 1966, Wiley. (G103.S7)

GENERAL WORLD ATLASES IN PRINT, 1972–1973, A COMPARATIVE ANALYSIS, 4th ed., Bowker. (Z6028.W27)

GLOSSARY OF GEOGRAPHICAL TERMS, 1961, Wiley. (G108.A2B7)

THE LITERATURE OF GEOGRAPHY, 1973, Linnet Books. General Orientation to geography. (Z6001.B74)

See also: B248.

■B241   GEOLOGY

BIBLIOGRAPHY AND INDEX OF GEOLOGY EXCLUSIVE OF NORTH AMERICA, 1933–, Geological Society. (Z6031.G4)

A DICTIONARY OF GEOLOGY, 3rd ed., 1967, Oxford. (QE5.C45)

THE ENCYCLOPEDIA OF GEOCHEMISTRY AND
ENVIRONMENTAL SCIENCES, 1972, Van Nostrand
Reinhold. (QE515.F24)
GEOLOGIC REFERENCE SOURCES: A SUBJECT AND
REGIONAL BIBLIOGRAPHY OF PUBLICATIONS AND
MAPS IN THE GEOLOGICAL SCIENCES, 1972, Scarecrow.
(QE1.C68)
GLOSSARY OF GEOLOGY, 3rd ed., 1972, American Geological
Institute. The most comprehensive dictionary on the subject.
Emphasis is on current meaning. (QE5.G37)
GUIDE TO GEOLOGIC LITERATURE, 1951, McGraw-Hill.
Hints on research and using libraries followed by various types
of geologic literature. (Z6031.P4)
THE LITERATURE OF GEOLOGY, 1953, Museum of Natural
History. Annotated list including government series and
maps. (Z6031.M36)
ROCK-FORMING MINERALS, by W. A. Deer, 5 vols., 1962–
1965, Wiley. Covers most important minerals of igneous,
metamorphic, and sedimentary rocks in detail. Gives struc-
ture, chemistry, optical, and physical properties, dis-
tinguishing features and paragenesis of each mineral.
Bibliographies. (QE364.D38)
See also: B248.

■B242 MATHEMATICS

BIBLIOGRAPHY
CURRENT INFORMATION SOURCES IN MATHEMATICS,
AN ANNOTATED GUIDE TO BOOKS AND
PERIODICALS, 1960–1972, 1973, Libraries Unlimited. This
up-dates the GUIDE TO THE LITERATURE IN
MATHEMATICS AND PHYSICS. (Z6651.D53)
GUIDE TO THE LITERATURE OF MATHEMATICS AND
PHYSICS, 2nd rev. ed., 1959, Dover. Includes methods of
research and lists of topics in the bibliography. (Z6651.P3)

DICTIONARIES
INTERNATIONAL DICTIONARY OF APPLIED
MATHEMATICS, 1960, Van Nostrand. Defines terms and
describes methods in the application of mathematics to fields
of physical sciences and engineering. (QA5.I5)
MATHEMATICS DICTIONARY, by G. James and R. C. James,

3rd ed., 1968, Van Nostrand. Very good, comprehensive, and clear. (QA5.J32)

TABLES

CRC HANDBOOK OF TABLES FOR MATHEMATICS, 4th ed., 1970, Chemical Rubber. A good practical handbook. (QA47.H32)

CRC STANDARD MATHEMATICAL TABLES, 22nd ed., 1974, CRC. (QA47.M315)

GUIDE TO TABLES IN MATHEMATICAL STATISTICS, 1962, Princeton. (Z6654.T3G7)

HANDBOOK OF MATHEMATICAL FUNCTIONS: WITH FORMULAS, GRAPHS, AND TABLES, rev. 1971, Govt. Printing Office. (QA3.V5)

HANDBOOK OF MATHEMATICAL TABLES AND FORMULAS, 5th ed., 1973, McGraw-Hill. (QA47.H32)

INTERNATIONAL CRITICAL TABLES, 7 vols., 1962–1963, McGraw-Hill. Standard comprehensive tables. (Q199.N32)

THE SMITHSONIAN PHYSICAL TABLES, 9th ed., 1956, U.S. Government Printing Office. (Q11.S7)

▪B243   MEDICAL DICTIONARY

CYCLOPEDIC MEDICAL DICTIONARY, by C. W. Taber, 12th ed., 1973, (revised frequently), Davis. Not merely definitions, but additional information in the various fields of medical practice, nursing, and allied subjects. (R121.T18)

MEDICAL ABBREVIATIONS, 3rd ed., 1971, F. A. Davis. (R123.S72)

▪B244   METALS AND METALLURGY

ASM REVIEW OF METAL LITERATURE, 1944– (annual), American Society for Metals. Comprehensive index. (TN1.A58)

A BRIEF GUIDE TO SOURCES OF METALS INFORMATION, 1973, Information Resources. Crammed full with useful information. (TN675.4H95)

ENCYCLOPEDIA OF MINERALS, 1974, Van Nostrand Reinhold. Covers all mineral species, with full color pictures. (QE355.R6)

A GUIDE TO INFORMATION SOURCES IN MINING, MINERALS AND GEOSCIENCES, 1965, Interscience. (Z7401.G83)

GUIDE TO METALLURGICAL INFORMATION, 2nd ed., 1965, Special Library Association. (Z6678.S65)

METALLURGICAL DICTIONARY, 1953, Reinhold. Concise definitions of essential terms. (TN609.H4)

METALS HANDBOOK, 5 vols., 8th ed., 1961–1971, American Society for Metals. Up-to-date information. (TA459.A5)

METALS REFERENCE BOOK, by C. J. Smithells, 3 vols., 4th ed., 1967, Butterworth. Summary of data relating to metallurgy and metal physics, presented in tables and diagrams. Bibliography. (TN671.S55)

MINERALS YEARBOOK, 1932–, U.S. Government Printing Office. General reviews followed by information on individual commodities. (TN23.U612)

▪B245 METEOROLOGY

GLOSSARY OF METEOROLOGY, 1959, American Meteorological Society. Defines every important term dealing with the atmosphere. (QC84.G55)

STANDARD DICTIONARY OF METEOROLOGICAL SCIENCES, 1971, McGill-Queen's. Updates the GLOSSARY OF METEOROLOGY. (QC854.P76)

WORLD CLIMATIC DATA, 1972, Climatic Data. A monumental compilation arranged by continent, then by country or state. (QC982.5.W4)

▪B246 MICROSCOPY

THE ENCYCLOPEDIA OF MICROSCOPY AND MICROTECHNIQUE, 1973, Reinhold. Bibliographies and good index. (QH203.G8)

▪B247 MICROBIOLOGY

ANNUAL REVIEW OF MICROBIOLOGY, 1947–, Annual Reviews, Inc. (QR1.A5)

HANDBOOK OF MICROBIOLOGY, 3 vols., 1973, CRC. Covers microorganisms themselves, constituents of microbiol cells, and tabulation of data on substances known to be formed by microorganisms. (QR6.C2)

ORGANIZATIONS
See: B251.

■B248 PERIODICAL INDEXES

AGRICULTURAL INDEX, 1916–1964, Wilson. Besides agriculture, it includes valuable material on heredity, biology, zoology, and forestry. Succeeded by BIOLOGICAL AND AGRICULTURAL INDEX, 1964–. (Z5073.A46)

AIR UNIVERSITY PERIODICAL INDEX, 1949–, Air University Library, Maxwell Air Force Base. Military and aeronautical. (Z5063.A2U8)

APPLIED SCIENCE AND TECHNOLOGY INDEX, 1958–, Wilson. By subject to some two hundred important periodicals. (Z7913.I7)

BIOLOGICAL ABSTRACTS, 1926–, University of Pennsylvania. Covers general biology and many related subjects. (QH301.B37)

BIOLOGICAL AND AGRICULTURAL INDEX, 1964–, Wilson. (Z5073.A45)

CHEMICAL ABSTRACTS, 1907–, American Chemical Society. Comprehensive; indispensable for locating current information in the field. (QD1.A511)

ENGINEERING INDEX, 1884–, Engineering Index, Inc. A valuable index, international in scope. Abstracts included. (Z5851.E62)

INDUSTRIAL ARTS INDEX, 1913–1957, Wilson. Covers engineering, chemistry, physics, geology, metallurgy, textiles, aeronautics, electronics, economics, business, insurance, and so forth. At the end of 1957, this was divided into two indexes: APPLIED SCIENCE AND TECHNOLOGY INDEX and BUSINESS PERIODICALS INDEX. (Z91.I7)

READERS' GUIDE TO PERIODICAL LITERATURE, 1900–, Wilson. General information. (AI3.R496)

SOCIAL SCIENCES AND HUMANITIES INDEX, 1907–, Wilson. Purely scientific and psychological materials were dropped from this index in 1955. This Index was divided into two separate titles in 1974. (AI3.R49)

■B249 PHYSICS

BIBLIOGRAPHY

GUIDE TO THE LITERATURE OF MATHEMATICS AND PHYSICS, 2nd rev. ed., 1959, Dover. Includes methods of

research and list of topics with a bibliography for each.
(Z6651.P3)

HOW TO FIND OUT ABOUT PHYSICS, 1965, Pergamon.
(Z7141.Y3)

PHYSICS LITERATURE, by R. H. Whitford, 2nd ed., 1968,
Scarecrow. Very useful guide. (Z7141.W47)

DICTIONARIES

CONCISE DICTIONARY OF PHYSICS AND RELATED
SUBJECTS, 1973, Pergamon. (QC5.T5)

DICTIONARY OF APPLIED PHYSICS, 5 vols., 1922–1923, Peter
Smith. Somewhat out-of-date but still useful. (QC5.G6)

ELSEVIER'S DICTIONARY OF GENERAL PHYSICS, 1962,
American Elsevier. (QC5.E46)

NEW DICTIONARY OF PHYSICS, by H. J. Gray, 2nd ed., 1974,
Longmans. Includes brief biographical information on
physicists. (QC5.G7)

DICTIONARY OF PHYSICS AND MATH ABBREVIATIONS,
SIGNS, AND SYMBOLS, 1965, Golden. (QC5.I5)

INTERNATIONAL DICTIONARY OF PHYSICS AND
ELECTRONICS, 2nd ed., 1961, Van Nostrand. Very useful.
(QC5.15)

DISSERTATIONS

DISSERTATIONS IN PHYSICS, 1861–1959, 1961, Stanford.
(Z7141.M3)

See also: B22.

GENERAL WORKS

AMERICAN INSTITUTE OF PHYSICS HANDBOOK, 3rd ed.,
1972, McGraw-Hill. A good authoritative source of information. (QC61.A5)

ENCYCLOPEDIC DICTIONARY OF PHYSICS, 9 vols., 1962, and
Suppls., Pergamon. Comprehensive and scholarly. Includes
many related subjects. (QC5.E52)

HANDBOOK OF PHYSICS, by E. U. Condon, 2nd ed., 1967,
McGraw-Hill. Standard work. (QC21.C7)

TABLES

HANDBOOK OF CHEMISTRY AND PHYSICS, 1914– (annual),
Chemical Rubber. Very valuable and useful. (QD65.H3)

See also: B238.

■B250   PHYSIOLOGY

ANNUAL REVIEW OF PHYSIOLOGY, 1939–, Annual Reviews, Inc. (BF30.A56)

SCIENTISTS
See: A5–A6, B227.

■B250a   SPACE FLIGHT

THE NEW SPACE ENCYCLOPEDIA; A GUIDE TO ASTRONOMY AND SPACE EXPLORATION, 2nd ed., 1974, Dulton. (TL788.S6)
See also: B221, B238.

■B251   SOCIETIES

HEALTH ORGANIZATIONS OF THE UNITED STATES, CANADA AND INTERNATIONALLY, 3rd ed., 1974, McGrath. Covers health and related fields. (R711.H4)
INTERNATIONAL SCIENTIFIC ORGANIZATIONS, 1962. U.S. Government Printing Office. Describes services, sources of information about, purpose, structure, and membership of each organization. Bibliography is annotated. (Q10.U5)
SCIENTIFIC AND TECHNICAL SOCIETIES OF THE UNITED STATES AND CANADA, 9th ed., 1972, National Academy of Sciences. Includes address, history, objects, membership, research funds, and so forth. (AS15.H3)
SCIENTIFIC SOCIETIES IN THE UNITED STATES, 3rd ed., 1965, M.I.T. (Q11.A1B3)

TECHNOLOGY
See: B238, B248.

■B252   ZOOLOGY

COLLEGIATE DICTIONARY OF ZOOLOGY, 1964, Ronald. (QL9.P4)

A DICTIONARY OF ZOOLOGY, by A. W. Leftwich, 1963, Van Nostrand. (QL9.L4)

GRZIMEK'S ANIMAL LIFE ENCYCLOPEDIA, 13 vols., 1972–1974, Van Nostrand Reinhold. Comprehensive and detailed. Good index. For the specialists. (QL3.G7813)

GUIDE TO THE LITERATURE OF THE ZOOLOGICAL SCIENCES, 1962, Burgess. Includes methods of research and publications in the field and related fields. (Z7991.S5)

THE INTERNATIONAL WILDLIFE ENCYCLOPEDIA, 20 vols., 1969–1970, Marshall Cavendish Corp. Well illustrated and highly informative. (QL9.B8)

PRIMATES, COMPARATIVE ANATOMY AND TAXONOMY, 8 vols., by W. C. Hill, 1953–1970, Wiley. A comprehensive work dealing with the structure, behavior, and classification of primates. (QL737.P9H53)

RAND McNALLY ATLAS OF WORLD WILDLIFE, 1973, Rand McNally. Emphasis is on higher vertebrates. (See Card Catalog)

B253–264 SOCIOLOGY AND ANTHROPOLOGY

■B253 BIBLIOGRAPHY

ANNOTATED GUIDE TO REFERENCE MATERIALS IN THE HUMAN SCIENCES, 1962, Asia Pub. House. A classified list with author and title indexes. (Z7164.S68M8)

CURRENT SOCIOLOGICAL RESEARCH, 1953– (annual), American Sociological Assoc. Lists research in progress. (H62.A57)

INTERNATIONAL BIBLIOGRAPHY OF SOCIAL AND CULTURAL ANTHROPOLOGY, 1955– (annual), Aldine. Comprehensive. (Z7161.I593)

INTERNATIONAL BIBLIOGRAPHY OF SOCIOLOGY, 1960– (annual), Aldine. Comprehensive. (Z7161.I594)

A READER'S GUIDE TO THE SOCIAL SCIENCES, edited by B. F. Hoselitz, Rev. ed., 1970, Free Press. Traces the development of the social sciences, giving noted works and their influence. (H61.H69)

SOURCES OF INFORMATION IN THE SOCIAL SCIENCES, 1973, ALA. (Z7161.W49)

■B254 BIOGRAPHY

AMERICAN MEN AND WOMEN OF SCIENCE: SOCIAL AND

BEHAVIORAL SCIENCES, 2 vols., 12th ed., 1973, Bowker. (Q141.A47)
See also: A5–A6.

◼B255 CITIES

COUNTY AND CITY DATA BOOK, 1967, U.S. Government Printing Office. Gives population figures and some other statistics. (HA202.A36)

THE MUNICIPAL YEAR BOOK, 1934– (annual), Inter-City Managers Association. Activities and statistical data of American cities. (JS344.C5)

◼B256 CRIMINOLOGY

BLOODLETTERS AND BADMEN: A NARRATIVE ENCYCLOPEDIA OF AMERICAN CRIMINALS FROM THE PILGRIMS TO THE PRESENT, 1973, Lippincott. Bibliography and index. (HV6785.N37)

DIRECTORY OF CORRECTIONAL INSTITUTIONS AND AGENCIES OF THE UNITED STATES OF AMERICA, CANADA, AND GREAT BRITAIN, (annual), American Correctional Association. (HV9463.A84)

ENCYCLOPEDIA OF CRIMINOLOGY, by V. C. Branham, 1949, Philosophical Library. Valuable for bibliographies. (HV6017.B7)

UNIFORM CRIME REPORTS FOR THE UNITED STATES 1930– (annual), Federal Bureau of Investigation. (HV6787.A3)

CURRENT INFORMATION
See: B18, B259.

◼B257 DICTIONARIES

DICTIONARY OF ANTHROPOLOGY, by C. Winick, 1970 (repr.), Greenwood. (GN11.W5)

DICTIONARY OF SOCIAL SCIENCE, edited by J. T. Zadrozny, 1959. Public Affairs. (H41.Z3)

DICTIONARY OF SOCIAL WELFARE, 1948, Social Sciences Pub. (HV12.Y6)

DICTIONARY OF SOCIOLOGY by H. P. Fairchild, 1970, Littlefield. (HM17.F3)

DICTIONARY OF SOCIOLOGY by Mitchell, 1968, Aldine. (HM17.M56)

A DICTIONARY OF THE SOCIAL SCIENCES, 1964, Free Press. (H41.G6)

A MODERN DICTIONARY OF SOCIOLOGY, 1969, Crowell. (HM17.T5)

■ B258 GENERAL WORKS

ANTHROPOLOGY TODAY, by A. L. Kroeber, 1953, University of Chicago. A symposium covering all phases of current anthropology. (GN4.I52)

ANNUAL REVIEW OF ANTHROPOLOGY, 1959–, Stanford University. (Z5112.B56)

CURRENT ANTHROPOLOGY, 1956, University of Chicago. A continuation of ANTHROPOLOGY TODAY. (GN.I52)

ENCYCLOPAEDIA OF RELIGION AND ETHICS, by J. Hastings, 13 vols., 1908–1927, Scribner's. Useful for primitive religions. (BL31.E44)

ENCYCLOPEDIA OF SOCIAL WORK, 2 vols., 1971, National Association of Social Workers. Covers articles, biographical sketches, statistics, and a directory of agencies. Successor to the SOCIAL WORK YEAR BOOK, 1920–1960. (HV35.S6)

ETHNOGRAPHIC ATLAS, 1967, U. of Pittsburgh. Summary of various items of ethnographic information on 862 societies. (GN405.M8)

A HUNDRED YEARS OF ANTHROPOLOGY, 1965, International U. A good starting point. (GN17.P4)

INTERNATIONAL ENCYCLOPEDIA OF THE SOCIAL SCIENCES, 17 vols., 1968, Macmillan. Comprehensive, good bibliographies and biographical material. (H40.A2I5)

See also: A1, B213, B238, B253, B259.

■ B259 PERIODICAL INDEXES

ABSTRACTS IN ANTHROPOLOGY, 1970–, Eastern New Mexico U. Covers Ethnology, Linquistics, Archaeology, and Physical Anthropology. (GN1.A15)

ESSAY AND GENERAL LITERATURE INDEX, 1900–, Wilson. Generally of some value in these areas. (AI3.E752)

HISTORICAL ABSTRACTS, 1955–, International Social Science Institute. Good for extensive research. (D299.H5)

THE NEW YORK TIMES INDEX, 1851–, The New York Times. Good for current news. (AI21.N44)

PUBLIC AFFAIRS INFORMATION SERVICE BULLETIN, 1915–, Public Affairs Information Service. Excellent. (Z7163.P9)

READERS' GUIDE TO PERIODICAL LITERATURE, 1900–, Wilson. General information. (AI3.R496)

SOCIAL SCIENCE ABSTRACTS, 1929–1933, Columbia University. Useful for historical topics. (H1.S56)

SOCIAL SCIENCES INDEX, 1974, Wilson. Very good. The new title of the former SOCIAL SCIENCES AND HUMANITIES INDEX.

SOCIOLOGICAL ABSTRACTS, 1952–, L. P. Chall. Valuable for any research. (HM1.S67)

■B260 POPULATION

CENSUS OF POPULATION, U.S. Government Printing Office. (See Card Catalog)
See also: A2–A3, B263.

■B261 SOCIAL REFORM

DICTIONARY OF AMERICAN SOCIAL REFORM, by L. Filler, 1963, Philosophical Library. Presents brief descriptions, definitions, references, phrases, personalities, events, and examples. (H41.F5)

■B262 SOCIAL WORK

ENCYCLOPEDIA OF SOCIAL WORK, 2 vols., 1971, National Association of Social Workers. Covers articles, biographical sketches, statistics, and a directory of agencies. (Successor to the SOCIAL WORK YEAR BOOK, 1920–1960.) (HV35.S6)

SOCIAL WORK REFERENCE AIDS, 1974, U. of Toronto. Annotated and arranged in subject categories. (See Card Catalog)
See also: B259.

■B263 STATISTICS

DEMOGRAPHIC YEARBOOK, 1948– (annual), United Nations. The best for worldwide vital statistics. (HA17.D45)

GUIDE TO U.S. GOVERNMENT STATISTICS, 1961, Documents Index. Arranged by departments and agencies with a detailed subject index. (Z7554.U5G8)
See also: B46, B158, B259.

■ **B264   UNITED NATIONS**

YEARBOOK OF THE UNITED NATIONS, 1947– (annual). United Nations. Summarizes activities, gives texts of documents, lists publications by or about the United Nations, and includes some biographies. (JX1977.A37A4)

See also: B259.

KEY TO PERIODICALS

KEY TO PERIODICALS

KEY TO PERIODICALS

Although periodical indexes are usually the best guide to current information, they are normally one to three months out of date. Therefore, it is necessary for the researcher to know which periodicals would be most helpful. This section is intended to be both selective, as well as, representative of standard periodicals found in a college library. The format is designed to help students find current information not yet included in periodical indexes. Because titles do not always convey the true content, they are listed under general subject field. Further subdivisions have been made where needed. Those periodicals reviewing books, drama, films, and records are so indicated. Each periodical title is followed by its frequency of publication and whatever the periodical reviews, if anything. More complete information may be found by consulting *Ulrich's Periodical Directory, Ayer's Directory of Newspapers and Periodicals.* (See B8) or Bill Katz *Magazines For Libraries*, an annotated list of approximately 4,500 titles (Z6941.K2). For information as to the location of periodical holdings in various libraries, consult the *Union List of Serials*, 5 vols., and its up-dating, *New Serial Titles*, 4 vols. (Z6945.U45).

GENERAL

BUYING GUIDE

CONSUMER REPORTS, monthly.
CONSUMER RESEARCH MAGAZINE, monthly. Record reviews.

CULTURE AND SOCIAL INTEREST

AMERICAN QUARTERLY, quarterly. Book reviews.
AMERICAN SCHOLAR, quarterly. Book reviews.

CURRENT EVENTS

FACTS ON FILE, weekly. Reviews.
MANCHESTER GUARDIAN WEEKLY, weekly. Book reviews.
NATION, weekly. Reviews: books, drama, films, records.
NEW REPUBLIC, weekly. Book reviews.
THE NEW YORK TIMES MAGAZINE, weekly.
NEWSWEEK, weekly. Book reviews.
TIME, weekly. Reviews: books, drama, movies, records.
U.S. NEWS AND WORLD REPORT, weekly.

GENERAL

ATLANTIC MONTHLY, monthly. Reviews: books and records.
BULLETIN OF THE ATOMIC SCIENTISTS, monthly. Book reviews.
EBONY, monthly.
HARPER'S MAGAZINE, weekly. Book reviews.
NEW YORKER, weekly. Reviews: art, books, movies, theater.
READER'S DIGEST, monthly.
SATURDAY EVENING POST, monthly (except Jan., June, Aug.)
SATURDAY REVIEW/WORLD, weekly. Reviews: books, films, plays.
TIMES LITERARY SUPPLEMENT, weekly. Book reviews.
VIRGINIA QUARTERLY REVIEW, quarterly. Book reviews.
YALE REVIEW, quarterly. Book reviews.

GEOGRAPHY

NATIONAL GEOGRAPHIC MAGAZINE, monthly.

RUSSIA

SOVIET LIFE, monthly.

SPEECHES

VITAL SPEECHES OF THE DAY, semimonthly.

ANTHROPOLOGY see **SOCIOLOGY AND ANTHROPO-LOGY**

ARCHAEOLOGY

GENERAL

AMERICAN ANTIQUITY, quarterly. Book reviews.
AMERICAN JOURNAL OF ARCHAEOLOGY, quarterly. Book reviews.
ANTIQUITY, quarterly. Book reviews.
ARCHAEOLOGY, quarterly. Book reviews.

ART

CONTEMPORARY

CRAFT HORIZONS, bimonthly.

GENERAL

ART NEWS, monthly (September through June); one issue for July, August.
ARTS MAGAZINE, monthly (Sept. through June). Reviews books, exhibitions.

HANDICRAFTS

CRAFT HORIZONS, bi-monthly. Book reviews.
EDUCATIONAL DEVELOPMENT, four per year. Book reviews.
HOBBIES, monthly. Book reviews.

HISTORY AND INTERPRETATION

ART BULLETIN, quarterly. Book reviews.

STUDY AND TEACHING

AMERICAN ARTIST, monthly (September through June). Book reviews.
ART EDUCATION, nine per year. Reviews: books, movies.
ART JOURNAL (formerly COLLEGE ART JOURNAL), quarterly. Book reviews.

SCHOOL ARTS MAGAZINE, 10 per year. Reviews: books, movies.

STUDIES IN ART EDUCATION, 3 times per year. Reviews: books, movies.

ASTRONAUTICS

GENERAL

JOURNAL OF THE ASTRONAUTICAL SCIENCES, quarterly. Book reviews.

SPACE WORLD, monthly. Book reviews.

SPACEFLIGHT, bimonthly. Book reviews.

ASTRONOMY

GENERAL

ASTRONOMICAL JOURNAL, ten per year.

ASTROPHYSICAL JOURNAL, bimonthly.

SKY AND TELESCOPE, monthly. Book reviews.

BIOLOGICAL SCIENCES

BOTANY

AMERICAN JOURNAL OF BOTANY, monthly.

ANNALS OF BOTANY, quarterly.

BOTANICAL GAZETTE, quarterly.

JOURNAL OF BIOLOGICAL CHEMISTRY, monthly.

PLANT PHYSIOLOGY, bimonthly.

ECOLOGY

ECOLOGY, quarterly. Book reviews.

ENTOMOLOGY

BULLETIN OF ENTOMOLOGICAL RESEARCH, quarterly.

ENTOMOLOGICAL SOCIETY OF AMERICA. ANNALS, bimonthly. Book reviews.

JOURNAL OF ECONOMIC ENTOMOLOGY, bimonthly.

EUGENICS

EUGENICS QUARTERLY, four per year. Book reviews.

GENERAL

AUDUBON MAGAZINE, bi-monthly. Book reviews.

BIOLOGICAL BULLETIN, bimonthly.

BIOSCIENCE, 24 per year. Book reviews.
NATURE (London), weekly. Book reviews.
QUARTERLY REVIEW OF BIOLOGY, quarterly. Book reviews.
SCIENCE, weekly.

PHYSIOLOGY

AMERICAN JOURNAL OF PHYSIOLOGY, monthly.
JOURNAL OF BIOLOGICAL CHEMISTRY, monthly.
JOURNAL OF GENERAL PHYSIOLOGY, bimonthly.
JOURNAL OF PHYSIOLOGY, three per year.

STUDY AND TEACHING

AMERICAN BIOLOGY TEACHER, monthly (August through May). Book reviews.
BSCS NEWSLETTER, four per year.

ZOOLOGY

ANATOMICAL RECORD, monthly. Book reviews.
JOURNAL OF EXPERIMENTAL BIOLOGY, quarterly.
JOURNAL OF EXPERIMENTAL ZOOLOGY, nine per year.
JOURNAL OF MORPHOLOGY, bimonthly.
JOURNAL OF ZOOLOGY, 3 vols. per year.

BUSINESS

ACCOUNTING

ACCOUNTING REVIEW, quarterly. Book reviews.
JOURNAL OF ACCOUNTANCY, monthly. Book reviews.

ADVERTISING AND SELLING

MARKETING/COMMUNICATIONS, monthly. Book reviews.
SALES MANAGEMENT, semimonthly.

BIBLIOGRAPHICAL

BUSINESS LITERATURE, irreg. (September through June).

FINANCE AND BANKING

BURROUGHS CLEARING HOUSE, monthly.
FEDERAL RESERVE BULLETIN, monthly.
JOURNAL OF FINANCE, quarterly. Book service.
WALL STREET JOURNAL, daily (except Saturday and Sunday).

FOREIGN TRADE

INTERNATIONAL COMMERCE WEEKLY, weekly.

GENERAL

BUSINESS WEEK, weekly.
CHANGING TIMES, monthly.
CONGRESSIONAL QUARTERLY SERVICE, weekly.
ECONOMIST (London), weekly. Book reviews.
HARVARD BUSINESS REVIEW, bimonthly.
JOURNAL OF COMMERCE, daily except Saturday and Sunday.
KIPLINGER WASHINGTON LETTER, weekly.

HISTORY

BUSINESS HISTORY REVIEW, quarterly. Book reviews.

INDUSTRY

FORTUNE, monthly.
See also: Production.

INVESTMENTS

FORBES, bi-monthly.
WALL STREET JOURNAL, daily except Saturday and Sunday.
See also: B68.

LABOR

INDUSTRIAL AND LABOR RELATIONS REVIEW, quarterly. Book reviews.
MONTHLY LABOR REVIEW, monthly.

MANAGEMENT

ADMINISTRATIVE MANAGEMENT, monthly.
DUN'S monthly. Reviews: books and business films.
MANAGEMENT REVIEW, monthly. Book reviews.
NATION'S BUSINESS, monthly. Book reviews.

MARKETING

JOURNAL OF MARKETING, quarterly. Book reviews.

OFFICE AIDS

ADMINISTRATIVE MANAGEMENT, monthly.

PERSONNEL

PERSONNEL, bi-monthly.
PERSONNEL JOURNAL, bimonthly. Book reviews.

PRODUCTION

PRODUCTION, monthly.
See also: Industry.

PUBLIC RELATIONS

PUBLIC RELATIONS JOURNAL, monthly. Book reviews.

PUBLISHING

PUBLISHERS WEEKLY, weekly.

RETAIL TRADE

JOURNAL OF RETAILING, quarterly. Book reviews.

STATISTICS

FEDERAL RESERVE BULLETIN, monthly.
SURVEY OF CURRENT BUSINESS, monthly.
TREASURY BULLETIN, monthly.

STOCK MARKET

AMERICAN INVESTOR, 10 per year.
BARRON'S, weekly.
WALL STREET JOURNAL, daily except Saturday and Sunday.

STUDY AND TEACHING

BALANCE SHEET, monthly (September through May).
BUSINESS EDUCATION FORUM, monthly (October through May). Book reviews.
JOURNAL OF BUSINESS EDUCATION, monthly (October through May). Book reviews.

CHEMISTRY

APPLIED CHEMISTRY

JOURNAL OF APPLIED CHEMISTRY, monthly.

BIOCHEMISTRY

BIOCHEMICAL JOURNAL, monthly.
JOURNAL OF BIOLOGICAL CHEMISTRY, monthly.

CHEMICAL ANALYSIS

ANALYTICAL CHEMISTRY, monthly. Book reviews.

GENERAL

CHEMICAL AND ENGINEERING NEWS, weekly. Book
reviews.
NATURE (London), weekly. Book reviews.

INDUSTRIAL

INDUSTRIAL AND ENGINEERING CHEMISTRY,
monthly.

ORGANIC

AMERICAN CHEMICAL SOCIETY JOURNAL,
semimonthly. Book reviews.
CHEMICAL SOCIETY JOURNAL, monthly.
JOURNAL OF ORGANIC CHEMISTRY, monthly.

PHYSICS AND CHEMISTRY

JOURNAL OF CHEMICAL PHYSICS, monthly.

RESEARCH

JOURNAL OF PHYSICAL CHEMISTRY, monthly.

STUDY AND TEACHING

JOURNAL OF CHEMICAL EDUCATION, monthly. Book
reviews.
JOURNAL OF RESEARCH IN SCIENCE TEACHING, 4 per
year. Book reviews.

THEORETICAL CHEMISTRY

CHEMICAL REVIEWS, bimonthly.

DRAMA

GENERAL

EDUCATIONAL THEATRE JOURNAL, quarterly. Book
reviews.
WORLD THEATER, bi-monthly. Book reviews.

ECONOMICS

FOREIGN TRADE

COMMERCE TODAY, fortn. Book reviews.

GENERAL

AMERICAN ECONOMIC REVIEW, 5 times per year. Book reviews.

CONGRESSIONAL QUARTERLY SERVICE, weekly.

ECONOMIST (London), weekly. Book reviews.

FORTUNE, monthly. Book reviews.

JOURNAL OF POLITICAL ECONOMY, bimonthly. Book reviews.

WALL STREET JOURNAL, daily except Saturday and Sunday.

HISTORY AND THEORY

ECONOMIC JOURNAL, quarterly. Book reviews.

JOURNAL OF ECONOMIC HISTORY, quarterly. Book reviews.

QUARTERLY JOURNAL OF ECONOMICS, quarterly.

INTERNATIONAL

JOURNAL OF INTERNATIONAL AFFAIRS, semiannual. Book reviews.

STATISTICS

ECONOMIC INDICATORS, monthly.

REVIEW OF ECONOMICS AND STATISTICS, quarterly. Book reviews.

SURVEY OF CURRENT BUSINESS, monthly.

EDUCATION

AUDIO-VISUAL AIDS

AUDIO-VISUAL JOURNAL, bi-monthly. Book reviews, film reviews.

MEDIA AND METHODS, monthly (Sept.–May). Book reviews.

CHILDREN

CHILDREN, bimonthly. Book reviews.

EXCEPTIONAL CHILDREN, monthly (October through May). Book reviews.

HORN BOOK MAGAZINE, bimonthly. Book reviews.

PARENTS MAGAZINE AND BETTER FAMILY LIVING, monthly. Book reviews.

See also: Elementary.

CURRICULUM

EDUCATIONAL LEADERSHIP, monthly (except June through September). Book reviews.

ELEMENTARY

ELEMENTARY SCHOOL JOURNAL, monthly (Oct.—May). Book reviews.
INSTRUCTOR, monthly (September through June).
JOURNAL OF EDUCATION, quarterly.
TEACHER, monthly (Sept.—May). Book reviews.

FEDERAL AND STATE INFORMATION

CONGRESSIONAL QUARTERLY SERVICE, weekly.

GENERAL

AMERICAN EDUCATION, monthly.
CALIFORNIA EDUCATION, monthly.
EDUCATION, monthly. Book reviews.
EDUCATION DIGEST, monthly (September through May).
EDUCATIONAL RECORD, quarterly.
PHI DELTA KAPPAN, monthly (Sept.—June). Book reviews.
REVIEW OF EDUCATIONAL RESEARCH, five per year.
TODAY'S EDUCATION, bi-monthly (Sept.—Mar.). Book reviews.

GUIDANCE AND COUNSELING

PERSONNEL AND GUIDANCE JOURNAL, monthly. (Sept.—June). Book reviews.

HIGHER

AAUP BULLETIN, quarterly.
THE CHRONICLE OF HIGHER EDUCATION, weekly (Bi-weekly, June—Sept.). Book reviews.
COLLEGE AND UNIVERSITY, quarterly.
INTELLECT, monthly (Oct.—May and summer issue).
JGE, quarterly. Book reviews.
JOURNAL OF HIGHER EDUCATION, monthly. Book reviews.

MANAGEMENT

AMERICAN SCHOOL BOARD JOURNAL, monthly. Book reviews.

SECONDARY

HIGH POINTS, irreg. Book reviews.

JOURNAL OF EDUCATION, bimonthly. Reviews: books and films.

NATIONAL ASSOCIATION OF SECONDARY SCHOOL PRINCIPALS, monthly (Sept.–May). Book reviews.

SCHOOL REVIEW, quarterly. Book reviews.

SOCIAL STUDIES, monthly. Book reviews.

SOCIOLOGICAL

SOCIOLOGY OF EDUCATION, monthly. Book reviews.

STATISTICAL

JOURNAL OF EDUCATIONAL RESEARCH, nine per year. Book reviews.

STUDY AND TEACHING

CONTEMPORARY EDUCATION, monthly. Book reviews.

IMPROVING COLLEGE AND UNIVERSITY TEACHING, quarterly. Book reviews.

EDUCATION FOR TEACHING, three per year. Book reviews.

HARVARD EDUCATIONAL REVIEW, quarterly. Book reviews.

JOURNAL OF TEACHER EDUCATION, quarterly. Book reviews.

QUARTERLY JOURNAL OF SPEECH, four per year. Book reviews.

VOCATIONAL

AMERICAN VOCATIONAL JOURNAL, monthly (September through May). Book reviews.

ENGINEERING

CHEMICAL

CHEMICAL AND ENGINEERING NEWS, weekly. Book reviews.

CHEMICAL ENGINEERING, fortnightly. Book reviews.

CHEMICAL ENGINEERING PROGRESS, monthly.

INDUSTRIAL AND ENGINEERING CHEMISTRY, monthly.

CIVIL

AMERICAN SOCIETY OF CIVIL ENGINEERS, PROCEEDINGS, consists of fifteen journals, irregular.
CIVIL ENGINEERING, monthly. Book reviews.

ELECTRICAL

ELECTRONICS, fortn. Book reviews.
IEEE PROCEEDINGS, monthly in three parts.
IEEE SPECTRUM, monthly.

GENERAL

ENGINEER (Buyers' Guide), weekly. Book reviews.
ENGINEERING, weekly. Book reviews.
ENGINEERING JOURNAL, monthly. Book reviews.
FRANKLIN INSTITUTE JOURNAL, monthly.
PLANT ENGINEERING, monthly. Book reviews.
U.S. NATIONAL BUREAU OF STANDARDS. *Technical News Bulletin*, monthly.

MECHANICAL

DIESEL EQUIPMENT SUPERINTENDENT, monthly.
HYDRAULICS AND PNEUMATICS, monthly.
INSTITUTION OF MECHANICAL ENGINEERS PROCEEDINGS, weekly.
IRON AGE, weekly.
MECHANICAL ENGINEERING, monthly. Book reviews.
POWER, monthly.
POWER ENGINEERING, monthly. Book reviews.

METALS

METAL PROGRESS, monthly. Book reviews.
METALS ENGINEERING QUARTERLY, quarterly.

STUDY AND TEACHING

JOURNAL OF ENGINEERING EDUCATION, monthly (October through June).

GEOGRAPHY

GENERAL

ASSOCIATION OF AMERICAN GEOGRAPHERS. *Annual*, quarterly. Book reviews.

ECONOMIC GEOGRAPHY, quarterly. Book reviews.
FOCUS, monthly (September through June).
GEOGRAPHICAL REVIEW, quarterly. Book reviews.
NATIONAL GEOGRAPHIC MAGAZINE, monthly.

STUDY AND TEACHING

JOURNAL OF GEOGRAPHY, monthly (September through May). Book reviews.

GEOLOGY

GENERAL

AMERICAN ASSOCIATION OF PETROLEUM GEOLOGISTS BULLETIN, monthly. Book reviews.
AMERICAN JOURNAL OF SCIENCE, monthly
AMERICAN MINERALOGIST, bimonthly. Book reviews.
ECONOMIC GEOLOGY, eight per year. Book reviews.
GEOLOGICAL SOCIETY OF AMERICA BULLETIN, monthly.
GEOSCIENCE ABSTRACTS (supersedes GEOLOGICAL ABSTRACTS), monthly.
JOURNAL OF GEOLOGY, bimonthly. Book reviews.

HISTORY

AMERICA

AMERICAN HERITAGE, bimonthly.
AMERICAN HISTORICAL REVIEW, bimonthly. Book reviews.
JOURNAL OF AMERICAN HISTORY, quarterly. Book reviews.
WILLIAM AND MARY QUARTERLY, quarterly. Book reviews.

ENGLAND

ENGLISH HISTORICAL REVIEW, quarterly. Book reviews.

EUROPE

JOURNAL OF MODERN HISTORY, quarterly. Book reviews.
SLAVIC REVIEW, quarterly. Book reviews.

GENERAL

AMERICAN HISTORICAL REVIEW, bimonthly. Book reviews.

HISTORY TODAY, monthly. Book reviews.

JOURNAL OF THE HISTORY OF IDEAS, quarterly. Book reviews.

LATIN AMERICA

AMERICAS, quarterly. Book reviews.

HISPANIC-AMERICAN HISTORICAL REVIEW, quarterly. Book reviews.

MEDIEVAL STUDIES

SPECULUM, quarterly. Book reviews.

NEGRO

JOURNAL OF NEGRO HISTORY, quarterly. Book reviews.

NEW ENGLAND

NEW ENGLAND QUARTERLY, quarterly. Book reviews.

RUSSIA

SLAVIC REVIEW, quarterly. Book reviews.

SOVIET LIFE, monthly.

STUDY AND TEACHING

SOCIAL STUDIES, monthly. Book reviews.

HOME ECONOMICS

BUYING GUIDES

CONSUMER RESEARCH MAGAZINE, monthly. Book reviews.

CONSUMER REPORTS, monthly.

COOKERY

FORECAST FOR HOME ECONOMICS, nine per year. Book reviews.

WHAT'S NEW IN HOME ECONOMICS, monthly (September through June). Book reviews.

GENERAL

AMERICAN HOME, monthly.

BETTER HOMES AND GARDENS, monthly.

GOOD HOUSEKEEPING, monthly.

HOUSE AND GARDEN, monthly.

JOURNAL OF HOME ECONOMICS, monthly (September through May). Book reviews.

LADIES' HOME JOURNAL, monthly.

VOGUE, semimonthly (monthly: January, June, July, December).

NUTRITION AND DIETETICS

AMERICAN DIETETIC ASSOCIATION JOURNAL, monthly. Book reviews.

JOURNAL OF NUTRITION, monthly.

LANGUAGES

FRENCH

FRENCH REVIEW, six per year. Book reviews.

ROMANTIC REVIEW, quarterly. Book reviews.

YALE FRENCH STUDIES, semiannual.

GENERAL

MODERN LANGUAGE QUARTERLY, quarterly. Book reviews.

MODERN LANGUAGE REVIEW, quarterly. Book reviews.

MODERN PHILOLOGY, quarterly. Book reviews.

PMLA Modern Language Association, 7 times a year.

GERMAN

GERMAN QUARTERLY, quarterly. Book reviews.

GERMANIC REVIEW, quarterly. Book reviews.

JOURNAL OF ENGLISH AND GERMANIC PHILOLOGY, quarterly. Book reviews.

MONATSHEFTE FUER DEUTSCHEN UNTERRICHT, quarterly. Book reviews.

SPANISH

HISPANIA, quarterly. Book reviews.

HISPANIC REVIEW, quarterly. Book reviews.

STUDY AND TEACHING

MODERN LANGUAGE JOURNAL, eight times a year. Book reviews.

LITERATURE

AUTHORS, beginning.

WRITER, monthly.

FICTION

MODERN FICTION STUDIES, quarterly.

GENERAL

ABSTRACTS OF ENGLISH STUDIES, ten per year.
ENCOUNTER, monthly. Book reviews.
ENGLISH, three per year. Book reviews.
ENGLISH STUDIES, bimonthly. Book reviews.
MODERN PHILOLOGY, quarterly. Book reviews.
PHILOLOGICAL QUARTERLY, quarterly. Book reviews.
PMLA Modern Language Association, 7 times a year.
REVIEW OF ENGLISH STUDIES, quarterly. Book reviews.

HISTORY AND CRITICISM

AMERICAN LITERATURE, bi-monthly (Nov.–May). Book reviews.

POETRY

POETRY, bi-monthly (Apr.–May). Book reviews.

SHAKESPEARE

SHAKESPEARE QUARTERLY, four per year. Book reviews.

STUDY AND TEACHING

COLLEGE ENGLISH, monthly (except June through September). Reviews: books, recordings.

MATHEMATICS

GENERAL

AMERICAN JOURNAL OF MATHEMATICS, four per year.
AMERICAN MATHEMATICAL MONTHLY, ten per year. Book reviews.
AMERICAN MATHEMATICAL SOCIETY BULLETIN, bi-monthly. Book reviews.
ANNALS OF MATHEMATICS, bimonthly.
JOURNAL OF MATHEMATICS AND PHYSICS, four per year.

JOURNAL OF RESEARCH (Section B), quarterly.
MATHEMATICAL REVIEWS, monthly.

STUDY AND TEACHING

ARITHMETIC TEACHER, monthly (October through May). Book reviews.

MATHEMATICS TEACHER, monthly (October through May). Book reviews.

SCHOOL SCIENCE AND MATHEMATICS, monthly (October through June). Book reviews.

MUSIC

DIRECTORS

CHORAL AND ORGAN GUIDE, ten per year. Reviews: books, music, records.

GENERAL

HIGH FIDELITY, monthly. Recording reviews (Incorporating MUSICAL AMERICA).

JAZZ

JAZZ JOURNAL, monthly. Reviews: books, records.

MODERN MUSIC

TEMPO, quarterly. Book reviews.

OPERA

OPERA NEWS, weekly (opera season); fortnightly (spring and fall). Reviews: books, music, records.

ORGANISTS AND PIANISTS

CLAVIER, six per year.
DIAPASON, monthly. Music reviews.

RECORDINGS

AMERICAN RECORD GUIDE, monthly. Reviews: books, records, tapes.

SACRED MUSIC

JOURNAL OF CHURCH MUSIC, monthly (September through June). Reviews: books, music.

STUDY AND TEACHING

AMERICAN MUSIC TEACHER, bi-monthly. Book reviews.

INSTRUMENTALIST, monthly (September through June). Reviews: books, films.

JOURNAL OF RESEARCH IN MUSIC EDUCATION, semiannual. Reviews: books, music.

MUSIC EDUCATORS JOURNAL, six per year. Reviews: books, music.

MUSIC JOURNAL, nine per year.

SCHOOL MUSICIAN, monthly (September through June). Reviews: books, films, records.

PHILOSOPHY see **RELIGION AND PHILOSOPHY**

PHYSICAL EDUCATION

COACHING

COACH AND ATHLETE, monthly (September through June). Book reviews.

MENTOR, monthly (August through May).

SCHOLASTIC COACH, monthly (September through June). Book reviews.

GENERAL

ATHLETIC JOURNAL, monthly (September through June). Book reviews.

JOURNAL OF HEALTH, PHYSICAL EDUCATION, RECREATION, monthly (Sept—June). Reviews: books, films.

PHYSICAL EDUCATION, three per year. Book reviews.

PHYSICAL EDUCATOR, four per year. Book reviews.

SPORTS ILLUSTRATED, weekly.

HYGIENE

AMERICAN JOURNAL OF PUBLIC HEALTH AND THE NATION'S HEALTH, monthly. Book reviews.

RESEARCH QUARTERLY, quarterly.

TODAY'S HEALTH, monthly. Book reviews.

RECREATION

PARKS AND RECREATION (formerly RECREATION), monthly (September through June). Reviews: books, films, records.

TENNIS
TENNIS, monthly. Book reviews.

PHYSICS

APPLIED

JOURNAL OF APPLIED PHYSICS, monthly. Book reviews.
PHILOSOPHICAL MAGAZINE, monthly. Book reviews.

ATOMIC ENERGY

NUCLEONICS, monthly. Book reviews.

ELECTRONICS

ELECTRONICS, fortn. Book reviews.

GENERAL

AMERICAN JOURNAL OF PHYSICS, monthly. Book reviews.
AMERICAN PHYSICAL SOCIETY BULLETIN, 7–8 per year.
NATURE (London), weekly. Book reviews.
PHYSICS TODAY, monthly. Book reviews.
REVIEW OF SCIENTIFIC INSTRUMENTS, monthly. Book reviews.
REVIEWS OF MODERN PHYSICS, quarterly.

OPTICS

OPTICAL SOCIETY OF AMERICA JOURNAL, monthly. Book reviews.

STUDY AND TEACHING

PHYSICS TEACHER, 9 per year. Reviews: books, films.

THEORETICAL

PHILOSOPHICAL MAGAZINE, monthly. Book reviews.
PHYSICAL REVIEW, weekly.

POLITICAL SCIENCE

CONGRESS

CONGRESSIONAL DIGEST, ten per year.
CONGRESSIONAL QUARTERLY SERVICE, weekly.
CONGRESSIONAL RECORD, daily when Congress is in session.

FOREIGN RELATIONS

DEPARTMENT OF STATE BULLETIN, weekly.
FOREIGN AFFAIRS, quarterly. Book list.

GENERAL

AMERICAN ACADEMY OF POLITICAL AND SOCIAL
SCIENCE ANNALS, bimonthly. Book reviews.
AMERICAN POLITICAL SCIENCE REVIEW, quarterly.
Book reviews.
ATLAS, monthly. Book reviews.
CURRENT HISTORY, monthly. Book reviews.
HEADLINE SERIES, bimonthly.
INTERNATIONAL CONCILIATION, bimonthly (except
July and August).
JOURNAL OF POLITICS, quarterly. Book reviews.
POLITICAL SCIENCE QUARTERLY, quarterly.

INTERNATIONAL AFFAIRS

JOURNAL OF INTERNATIONAL AFFAIRS, semiannual.
Book reviews.
UNITED NATIONS MONTHLY CHRONICLE, monthly.

INTERNATIONAL LAW

AMERICAN JOURNAL OF INTERNATIONAL LAW,
quarterly.

PUBLIC OPINION

PUBLIC OPINION QUARTERLY, quarterly. Book reviews.

PSYCHOLOGY

CHILDREN

CHILD DEVELOPMENT, quarterly.
CHILD STUDY JOURNAL, quarterly.
CHILDREN, bimonthly.

EXPERIMENTAL

AMERICAN JOURNAL OF PSYCHOLOGY, quarterly.
Book reviews.
JOURNAL OF EXPERIMENTAL PSYCHOLOGY,
monthly.

GENERAL

AMERICAN PSYCHOLOGIST, monthly.
PSYCHOLOGY TODAY, monthly. Book reviews.

STUDY AND TEACHING

JOURNAL OF CONSULTING PSYCHOLOGY, bimonthly.
Review tests.
JOURNAL OF EDUCATIONAL PSYCHOLOGY, bimonthly. Book reviews.

THEORY AND RESEARCH

JOURNAL OF ABNORMAL PSYCHOLOGY, bimonthly.
JOURNAL OF PERSONALITY AND SOCIAL
PSYCHOLOGY, monthly.
PSYCHOLOGICAL REVIEW, bimonthly.

RELIGION AND PHILOSOPHY

BIBLE

JOURNAL OF BIBLICAL LITERATURE, quarterly. Book
reviews.

CATHOLIC

AMERICA, weekly. Reviews: books, drama, films.
COMMONWEAL, weekly. Book reviews.

CHURCH-STATE RELATIONS

JOURNAL OF CHURCH AND STATE, 3 times per year.
Book reviews.

EDUCATION

CHRISTIAN SCHOLAR, quarterly. Book reviews.
INTERNATIONAL JOURNAL OF RELIGIOUS
EDUCATION, eleven per year. Book reviews.
RELIGIOUS EDUCATION, bimonthly. Book reviews.

GENERAL

CHRISTIAN CENTURY, weekly. Book reviews.
CHRISTIANITY AND CRISIS, fortnightly.
CHRISTIANITY TODAY, fortnightly. Book reviews.
CTM, 5 per year. Book reviews.
ETHICS, quarterly. Book reviews.
EVANGELICAL QUARTERLY, quarterly. Book reviews.

HIBBERT JOURNAL, quarterly. Book reviews.
HIS MAGAZINE, nine per year.
INTERPRETATION, quarterly. Book reviews.
JOURNAL OF BIBLE AND RELIGION, quarterly. Book reviews.
JOURNAL OF PHILOSOPHY, fortnightly. Book reviews.
PASTORAL PSYCHOLOGY, monthly (September through June).
PHILOSOPHICAL REVIEW, quarterly.
THEOLOGY TODAY, quarterly. Book reviews.

HISTORY

CHURCH HISTORY, quarterly. Book reviews.
JOURNAL OF RELIGION, quarterly. Book reviews.

JEWISH

COMMENTARY, monthly. Book reviews.

MISSIONS

INTERNATIONAL REVIEW OF MISSIONS, quarterly. Book reviews.

SCIENCE

CURRENT NEWS

SCIENCE NEWS, weekly. Book reviews.

GENERAL

BULLETIN OF THE ATOMIC SCIENTISTS, monthly (except July and August). Book reviews.
DAEDALUS, quarterly.
ENDEAVOUR, 3 per year. Book reviews.
NATURAL HISTORY (incorporating NATURE MAGAZINE), monthly (October through May); bimonthly (June through September). Book reviews.
NATURE (London), weekly. Book reviews.
SCIENCE, weekly. Book reviews.
SCIENCE DIGEST, monthly.
SCIENTIFIC AMERICAN, monthly. Book reviews.

HISTORY

ANNALS OF SCIENCE, quarterly.
ISIS, quarterly. Book reviews.

STUDY AND TEACHING

JOURNAL OF COLLEGE SCIENCE TEACHING, quarterly. Reviews: books, films.

SOCIOLOGY AND ANTHROPOLOGY

CRIMINOLOGY

JOURNAL OF CRIMINAL LAW, CRIMINOLOGY AND POLICE SCIENCE, quarterly. Book reviews.

GENERAL

AMERICAN ANTHROPOLOGIST, bimonthly. Book reviews.
AMERICAN BEHAVIORAL SCIENTIST, bimonthly. Book reviews.
AMERICAN JOURNAL OF SOCIOLOGY, bimonthly. Book reviews.
AMERICAN SOCIOLOGICAL REVIEW, bimonthly. Book reviews.
CURRENT ANTHROPOLOGY, 5 per year. Book reviews.
CURRENT SOCIOLOGY, 3 per year.
DAEDALUS, quarterly.
PRACTICAL ANTHROPOLOGY, bimonthly. Book reviews.
SOCIAL FORCES, quarterly. Book reviews.
SOUTHWESTERN JOURNAL OF ANTHROPOLOGY, quarterly.

MARRIAGE

JOURNAL OF MARRIAGE AND THE FAMILY, quarterly. Book reviews.

RACE

PHYLON, quarterly. Book reviews.
RACE, quarterly. Book reviews.

RURAL

RURAL SOCIOLOGY, quarterly. Book reviews.

SOCIAL ISSUES

JOURNAL OF SOCIAL ISSUES, quarterly.
SOCIAL PROBLEMS, quarterly.
SOCIAL WORK, quarterly. Book reviews.

APPENDIX

■ BOOK REVIEW DIGEST

This work indexes reviews of current books which appear in periodicals and newspapers.

Author's name ──────────────▶ BERKNER, LLOYD VIEL, ed.
                              ▶ Science in space ed. by Lloyd V.
Title ──────────   Berkner [and] Hugh Odishaw.
                                458p il $7 McGraw   523.1 Outer
                                space   61-9772

"An anthology in which 20 contributors describe what has been learned by the firing of rockets and satellites, what the U.S. plans to investigate via future shots and what is involved in such programs as placing a man on the moon." (San Francisco Chronicle) Chapter bibliographies. Indexes.

Bookmark 21:9 O '61 10w

" 'Science in Space' is a collection of 20 review articles by some of the most outstanding names in American science and was prepared under the guidance of the Space Science Board of the National Academy of Sciences.... Highly recommended for university, college and public libraries, except the very small." J. K. Lucker

Plus (+) and minus (−) signs are included to indicate favor or disfavor of the entire review. Dropped in 1963.

+Library J 86:2328 Je 15 '61 190w

"These 20 authoritative, expert reviews by noted scientists are primarily for perceptive research workers, but they should also be of interest to intelligent general readers concerned about the national space effort.... A notable work."

+N Y New Tech Bks 46:132 S '61

"Much of the book is too technical for the average reader, requiring a familiarity with higher mathematics, but on the other hand, much of it is not too technical, and all of it offers an exact picture of where we stand at the moment vis-a-vis the dark and empty depths of space." J. W.

+ San Francisco Chronicle p26 Je 11 '61 140w

SOURCE: *Book Review Digest*, April, 1962, Vol. 58, No. 2, p. 10.

Subject of book

Descriptive note by editor of *Book Review Digest*

Source given, but no excerpt

Digests of reviews, giving source directly below
excerpt (Title, vol., page, date, and number of words)

■ CUMULATIVE BOOK INDEX

This is a comprehensive list of current books in the English language listed by author, title, and subject.

A cross reference
referring from
a heading not
used to one
that is used. ──────────→ Edlin, Herbert Leeson
(tr) See Rytz, W. Flowers in color

Edmunds, Murrell, 1898- ──────────
Moon of my delight; a play in 3 acts, 144p $6 '60 Yoseloff 60-10846

Ednie, H. H. See Paterson, W. E. jt. auth.

Educating in five dimensions. Beaumont, H. W. pa 7s 6d Reed

Title ──────────→ Educating the gifted. Fleege, U. H. ed. pa $2 DePaul univ. Dept. of educ, 25 E. Jackson blvd, Chicago 4

Subject ──────────→ Education
Birmingham, England. University. Institute of education. Education in an age of technology. pa 9s '60 The institute. Birmingham 15, England
International conference on public education, 1960. [Proceedings of the] Conference [convened by UNESCO and the Int. bur. of educ] countries represented: Afghanistan [and others] pa $1.75 '61 Columbia univ. press; pa 8s 6d H.M.S.O; pa 6fr Int. bur. of educ; UNESCO
Logue, G. Aims and methods of Western education. 21s '60 Juta
Russell, W. H. Introduction to public education. $6 '60 Educ. pubs (St Louis)

List of books
on Education ──────────→ Aims and objectives
Brameld, T. B. H. Education for the emerging age. $5 '61 Harper
Bibliography
Silvey, H. M. ed. Master's theses in education, 1959-60. $6.50 '60 Res. publications, Cedar Falls, Iowa
Congresses
Educational conference, 1959. Curriculum planning to meet tomorrow's needs. pa $2 '60 Am. council on educ.
Curricula ──────────
Association for supervision and curriculum development. Yearbook, 1961. $4 '61 Nat. educ.

Author entries give the most detailed data. (Data includes
the author, title, price, edition, publisher, number of
pages, date of issue, and Library of Congress card order
number.)

Subheading under Education

■ ESSAY AND GENERAL LITERATURE INDEX

Indexes works and parts of works of a general nature that appear in books.

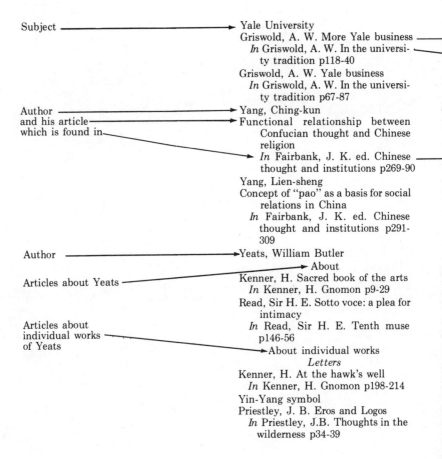

Subject ⟶ Yale University
Griswold, A. W. More Yale business ⟶
   In Griswold, A. W. In the universi-
   ty tradition p118-40
Griswold, A. W. Yale business
   In Griswold, A. W. In the universi-
   ty tradition p67-87

Author ⟶ Yang, Ching-kun
and his article ⟶ Functional relationship between
which is found in ⟶   Confucian thought and Chinese
   religion
   In Fairbank, J. K. ed. Chinese ⟶
   thought and institutions p269-90
Yang, Lien-sheng
Concept of "pao" as a basis for social
   relations in China
   In Fairbank, J. K. ed. Chinese
   thought and institutions p291-
   309

Author ⟶ Yeats, William Butler
   ⟶ About
Articles about Yeats ⟶ Kenner, H. Sacred book of the arts
   In Kenner, H. Gnomon p9-29
Read, Sir H. E. Sotto voce: a plea for
   intimacy
Articles about   *In* Read, Sir H. E. Tenth muse
individual works ⟶   p146-56
of Yeats ⟶ About individual works
   Letters
Kenner, H. At the hawk's well
   In Kenner, H. Gnomon p198-214
Yin-Yang symbol
Priestley, J. B. Eros and Logos
   In Priestley, J.B. Thoughts in the
   wilderness p34-39

Author and title of article on the subject: Yale University

Author and title of book in which the article appears.

The complete information on the author and title will be found in the back of each index.

SOURCE: *Essay and General Literature Index*, June, 1958, p. 121.

■ THE NEW YORK TIMES INDEX

Although an index to one particular newspaper, it serves as an index to all newspaper items of general interest, since all newspapers publish news items at about the same time.

Cross references referring from headings not used to those used. →

MARITAL Relations. See Families.

MARITIME Assn, Pacific. See Stevedoring—US—W Coast Ja 5

MARITIME Law. See Ships—Accidents, C. Sadikoglu par. Ships—Gen Ja 15

MARITIME Union, National. See Ry Council, NY Harbor

MARITIME Workers Union, International. See Ships—Regis Ja 14

Personal name → MARKEL, Edward Son Howard to wed L. Macy, Ja 15,92:2

MARKETING and Merchandising. See US—Econ, production, distribution, consumption par. Other geog heads (subdiv Econ where subdivided). Related subjects, eg, Advertising, Retail Stores, Sales. Commodity, co and indus names

MARKETING Assn, American. See US Econ, production par Ja 11

MARKS, Morris A. See Valley Natl Bank

MARLOW, W. F. See Carbon Ja 11, 15

MARQUETTE Cement Mfg Co. See N Amer Cement.

MARQUIS-Who's Who Inc. See Books—Awards Ja 11

Subject heading → MARRIAGES, See related subjects, eg, Divorce, Families. Personal names GB: Sir John Wolfenden holds Brit still prejudiced about interracial marriages, article, Ch of Eng pub, Ja 13,5:5. USSR: O Caruthers article, Moscow's 'Store for Newlyweds'; illus, Ja 15, VI, p42. UAR: major changes in Egyptian laws proposed to give new rights to Moslem women, Ja 15,19:1. US: Episc Soc for Cultural and Racial Unity upholds interracial marriages, Ja 11,16:4

MARTIN, (Repr) Dave. See Sugar, US (gen) par Ja 7

MARTIN, Mary. Daughter Heller to wed G Stephens, Ja 8,88:1

MARTIN, (Chmn) Wm McChesney Jr. See Credit—Bank Ja 12 in Ja 6 par

Summary of news item

Some cross references give date of entry.

Articles on marriages giving dates,
pages, and column numbers.

Summary of news item

◼ PUBLIC AFFAIRS INFORMATION SERVICE BULLETIN

Indexes on a selective basis, periodicals, books, documents, pamphlets, and other publications.

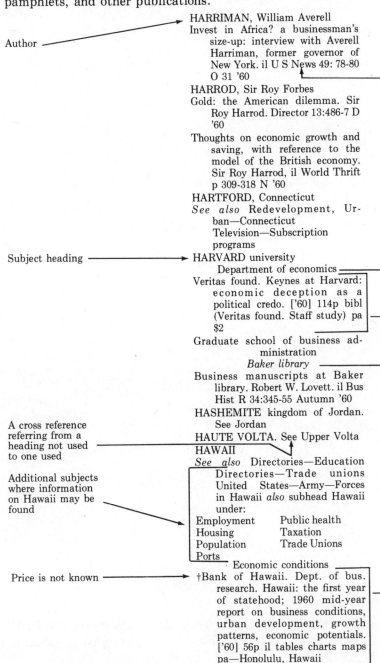

Author

HARRIMAN, William Averell
Invest in Africa? a businessman's size-up: interview with Averell Harriman, former governor of New York. il U S News 49: 78-80 O 31 '60

HARROD, Sir Roy Forbes
Gold: the American dilemma. Sir Roy Harrod. Director 13:486-7 D '60

Thoughts on economic growth and saving, with reference to the model of the British economy. Sir Roy Harrod, il World Thrift p 309-318 N '60

HARTFORD, Connecticut
See also Redevelopment, Urban—Connecticut
Television—Subscription programs

Subject heading

HARVARD university
Department of economics
Veritas found. Keynes at Harvard: economic deception as a political credo. ['60] 114p bibl (Veritas found. Staff study) pa $2

Graduate school of business administration
Baker library
Business manuscripts at Baker library. Robert W. Lovett. il Bus Hist R 34:345-55 Autumn '60

HASHEMITE kingdom of Jordan. See Jordan

A cross reference referring from a heading not used to one used

HAUTE VOLTA. See Upper Volta
HAWAII
See also Directories—Education
Directories—Trade unions
United States—Army—Forces in Hawaii also subhead Hawaii under:

Additional subjects where information on Hawaii may be found

Employment   Public health
Housing   Taxation
Population   Trade Unions
Ports

Economic conditions

Price is not known

†Bank of Hawaii. Dept. of bus. research. Hawaii: the first year of statehood; 1960 mid-year report on business conditions, urban development, growth patterns, economic potentials. ['60] 56p il tables charts maps pa—Honolulu, Hawaii

⟶ Periodical

⟶ Subheading under Harvard U.

⟶ Booklet

⟶ Subdivision under Graduate School of . . .

⟶ Booklet

SOURCE: *Bulletin of the Public Affairs Information Service.*
Feb. 18, 1961, Vol. 47, No. 20, p. 168.

Dewey Decimal Classification: Examples

The Dewey Decimal Classification is basically a numerically arranged system. The number-examples above each stand for a specific subject. These may be further subdivided, as in the case of 230 Christian theology, by using the decimal point 232.9 Life of Jesus Christ. This classification number is placed on the spine of a book along with an author-number consisting of Letters and Numbers. The author-number places the book on the shelf alphabetically within a specific classification. Like books are thus brought together in one place on the library shelves.

000–099 GENERAL WORKS

010   Bibliography—lists of books
020   Library science
030   General encyclopedias
070   Journalism
080   Collected works

100–199 PHILOSOPHY

100–109   General works
140   Philosophical topics
150   Psychology
160   Logic
170   Ethics
180–190   Philosophers

200–299 RELIGION

200–209   General works
210   Natural theology
220   Bible
230   Christian Theology
    232.9   Life of Jesus Christ
260   Christian church and its work
    266   Missions
270   History of Christianity
280   Christian churches and sects
290   Other religions

300–399 SOCIAL SCIENCES

300–309 General works
310 Statistics
320 Political science
330 Economics
340 Law
350 Government
370 Education
390 Customs and folklore

400–499 LANGUAGES

400-409 General works
423 Dictionaries

500–599 SCIENCE

500–509 General works
510 Mathematics
520 Astronomy
530 Physics
540 Chemistry
550 Geology
570 Biology
580 Botany
590 Zoology

600–699 TECHNOLOGY

600–609 General works
610 Medical science
620 Engineering
640 Home economics
650 Business
657 Accounting
658 Business and industrial management
660 Chemical technology

700–799 FINE ARTS AND RECREATION

700–709 General works
720 Architecture
740 Drawing

750   Painting
780   Music
790   Recreation and sports

800–899   LITERATURE

800–809   General works
809   History and criticism
810   American literature
811   Poetry
812   Drama
813   Fiction
814   Essays
820   English literature

900–999   HISTORY

900–909   General works
910   Travel and geography
920   Biography, collections
    921–928   Individuals
930   Ancient history
940   Europe
942   England
947   Russia
950   Asia
960   Africa
970   North America
971   Canada
973   United States
980   South America
990   Oceanic and Polar regions

Library of Congress Classification: Examples

The Library of Congress Classification differs from the Dewey Classification in that it is basically an alphabetically arranged system. A single letter or combination of letters stand for a specific subject field. These may be further subdivided numerically similar to that of the Dewey System, then by using the decimal point. This is followed by the author-number. For example this book's classification number (call number) is:

Z
1035.1
.M6

Likewise, the books classified according to the Library of Congress System brings books of like nature together in one place on the library shelves.

A   GENERAL WORKS

    AE   Encyclopedias (general)
    AI   Indexes (general)
    AY   Yearbooks (general)

B   PHILOSOPHY—RELIGION

    B—   BJ   Philosophy
         B   Collection. History.
         BC   Logic
         BF   Psychology
         BJ   Ethics
    BL—   BX   Religion
         BP   Christianity
         BS   Bible and Exegesis
         BX   Special sects

C   HISTORY—AUXILIARY SCIENCES

    CB   History of civilization

CC   Antiquities (general). Archaeology.
CT   Biography

D   HISTORY AND TOPOGRAPHY (except America)

D   General History
DA   Great Britain
DK   Russia
DS   Asia
DT   Africa

E— NORTH AND SOUTH AMERICA

G   GEOGRAPHY—ANTHROPOLOGY

G   Geography (general)
GN   Anthropology
GV   Sports and amusements. Games.

H   SOCIAL SCIENCES

H   Social sciences (general)
HA   Statistics
HB— HJ   Economics
    HB   Economic theory
    HF   Commerce
HM—HX   Sociology
    HQ   Family, marriage, home
    HT   Communities. Races.
    HX   Socialism. Communism.

J   POLITICAL SCIENCE

JC   Political science
JF— JX   Constitutional history and administration.

K   LAW

L   EDUCATION

LA	History of education
LB	Theory and practice of education. Teaching.
LD– LT	Universities and colleges

M   MUSIC

M	Music
ML	Literature of music
MT	Musical instruction and study

N   FINE ARTS

NA	Architecture
ND	Painting
NK	Art applied to industry

P   LANGUAGE AND LITERATURE

PA	Classical languages and literatures
PB– PH	Modern European languages
PJ– PL	Oriental languages and literatures
PN– PZ	Literature
PN	Literary history and collections (general)
PR	English literature
PS	American literature
PZ	Fiction and juvenile literature

Q   SCIENCE

Q	Science (general)
QA	Mathematics
QC	Physics
QD	Natural history. Biology.
QL	Zoology

R MEDICINE

RA Hygiene
RT Nursing

S AGRICULTURE—PLANT AND ANIMAL INDUSTRY

SD Forestry
SK Hunting sports

T TECHNOLOGY

TA–TH Engineering and building group
TL Motor vehicles. Aeronautics.

U MILITARY SCIENCE

V NAVAL SCIENCE

Z BIBLIOGRAPHY

TITLE INDEX

TITLE INDEX

SUBJECT INDEX

SUBJECT INDEX

(The numerals listed in the SUBJECT INDEX refer to the code numbers in the text and not to page numbers.)